Alien Technology
Coping with Modern Mysteries

Ananda Mitra

SAGE
www.sagepublications.com
Los Angeles • London • New Delhi • Singapore • Washington DC

First published in 2010 by

SAGE Publications India Pvt Ltd
B1/I-1 Mohan Cooperative Industrial Area
Mathura Road, New Delhi 110 044, India
www.sagepub.in

SAGE Publications Inc
2455 Teller Road
Thousand Oaks, California 91320, USA

SAGE Publications Ltd
1 Oliver's Yard
55 City Road
London EC1Y 1SP, United Kingdom

SAGE Publications Asia-Pacific Pte Ltd
33 Pekin Street
#02-01 Far East Square
Singapore 048763

Published by Vivek Mehra for SAGE Publications India Pvt Ltd, typeset in 11.5/13.5 pt Baskerville MT by Innovative Processors, New Delhi and printed at Chennai Micro Print (P) Ltd., Chennai.

Library of Congress Cataloging-in-Publication Data
Mitra, Ananda, 1960-
    Alien technology : coping with modern mysteries/Ananda Mitra.
        p. cm.
    Includes bibliographical references and index.
    1. Technological innovations—Social aspects. 2. Technological innovations —Psychological aspects. 3. Alienation (Social psychology) I. Title.

HM846.M58   303.48'3—dc22   2010   2010033658
ISBN: 978-81-321-0466-7 (PB)

The SAGE Team: Elina Majumdar, Sonalika Rellan, and
                                Sanjeev Kumar Sharma

*This book is dedicated to our ancient ancestors
who looked at a circular piece of stone and wondered what to do
with it, and then figured out the usefulness of the wheel.*

Contents

Preface

Apple Corporation, who gave the world the iPod and later the iPhone, had hoped to sell 10 million iPhones by the end of 2008. They nearly reached that goal. In other words, there are 10 million people in the world who now own an iPhone. Yet the iPhone is a complex tool. Its function as a phone is only the tip of the iceberg of functions that the iPhone can be made to do. Indeed a cottage industry has grown up around this tool with numerous people composing simple computer programs that will allow the user of the iPhone to do a myriad of tasks from finding a restaurant in New York to doing a Ganesh Puja to worship the Hindu God. There were about 10,000 such programs, or applications, that were available to the iPhone user in 2008 and the numbers continue to grow. The iPhone is also one of the numerous tools, from the digital camera to the fuel-efficient family car, that have flooded the technology marketplace all over the world. This has been the trend in the developed nations of the West since World War II and has now become the trend in countries like China and India where large populations now have the desire and capability of owning these tools. Ownership is, however, not an indicator of use.

This book deals with the condition that the owner of a tool might not actually be using the tool to its full and possible potentials. In an absurd extension of full functionality, one would think that the owner of the iPhone would actually have all 10,000 applications installed on the gadget. But even if one were not to go to that extreme, it is often the case that a large portion of users remain distant from their gadgets. The tools become inscrutable and alien, and the level of alienation is only increased as the tools become more sophisticated. This book is about the different possible levels of alienation of the user from the tools that an individual might be compelled to use. This book is also about the ways in which overcoming the alienation can allow people to become better and empowered users of the gadgets that might have appeared to be mysterious at one time.

Through the process of empowerment it is possible to deploy the tools in a manner that could provide a voice to the people using the tool. However, that becomes a political argument as made by authors like Roger Silverstone in talking about the relatively restricted scope of media alone in the book *Media and Morality*. Silverstone suggests that one needs to understand the power of media technologies and realize its empowering or disempowering potentials. To be sure, some tools can offer that space for the marginal to become empowered, but the purpose of my book is not to look for the ways in which tools empower people, but to demonstrate that a *pre-condition* for empowerment of any form is to overcome the intrinsic alienation that people feel with respect to the tools themselves.

I would hope that after reading this book there would be a moment of introspection to consider where we stand with respect to the gadgets and machines that have become a part of our lives. The response cannot be what the textile artisans called Luddites did in York in 1811 when they protested the arrival of textile mills by attacking and damaging the factories, but the response must involve seeking out appropriate information that would reduce the alienation from the tools so that we are not enslaved by the tools but gain control on the way in which we must use the tools to add to our quality of life.

Acknowledgements

I would like to thank a group of people who made this book possible. My gratitude firstly goes to my family in America and India who provided support and balance to my writing life. Appreciation also goes to my friends in Winston-Salem and to my colleagues at Wake Forest University who provided the encouragement throughout the entire process of writing this book. A word of thanks also goes to Elina Majumdar of SAGE Publications who provided the encouragement and criticism over coffee at several meetings in Delhi. Finally, I have to thank my wife Swati and my son Srijoy for allowing me to squander on gadgets and toys that all played a part in conceptualizing the idea of alien technology.

The Law of Technological Alienation

I write this sentence on my notebook computer sitting in a plane circling over eastern Virginia in the United States. Our plane has been put on a "holding pattern" due to a storm at Washington's Dulles International Airport. I, or any other passenger on the plane, can do very little to control our destinies till we are in the terminal at the airport. In fact, I am completely dependant on a series of interconnected technological systems that include the engineering of the aircraft and the satellite systems that provide weather information to the Air Traffic Controllers at the airport. My plane, just like numerous other planes, is rapidly making the apparently open skies uncomfortably crowded. Yet, most passengers on these planes have only a passing acquaintance with the technology on which their life depends. Such are the alien technologies that surround and control us.

This book is about the way in which we have increasingly been alienated from the technology around us. The price of this alienation could be as tragic as the death by suicide of teenagers prescribed antidepressant drugs without understanding how the chemicals affect the body while the reward of the alienation is the magical trust we place in the fact that my plane, and all the other planes, will eventually land safely in Dulles in near-zero visibility. The focus here is on the consequence of becoming increasingly distant from the technologies in terms of knowing what makes the tools tick.

THINKING ABOUT TECHNOLOGY

Before it is possible to explore the notion of distancing from technology, it is necessary to consider a specific way of thinking about the idea of technology as a tool. If one were to look at the origin of the word, one would find that the word "technology" is derived from the Greek word "technikos" which really described the combination of being artistic and professional at the same time. From a very early point the idea of technology referred to the moment when the artist/craftsman became a professional and produced something that was no longer art, but an artefact. Now, moving forward to the age of Wikipedia, the free encyclopedia on the Internet, one would find technology defined as the, "use of the engineered product". The pointer is back to the idea of an artefact, a product—a tool. Using that as the starting point it can be argued that the notion of technology and the production and application of tools are intimately related. Eventually, we invest in tools offered by technology because we make an intrinsic assumption that these artefacts would allow us to do something better or in an easier way.

The work of tilling land provides a good illustration of the way in which technology can be expected to work. To make the land ready for cultivation it is necessary to be able to soften the top soil, aerate it, hydrate it, and then plant seeds. Thereafter, it is necessary to feed the seed, the seedling, and the plant and eventually harvest the produce which provides the essential element for human survival—food. From the beginning of the agricultural process all these tasks required some form of human labor. The tilling of land required the use of a plow, which could be pulled by hand. Clearly, this was not an efficient process and required tremendous effort, time, and resources. It also required a series of skills including metal working or wood carving which would be used to produce the plow. Thereafter, human creativity stepped in and the plow was incrementally improved, and methods were devised to use the labor of a domesticated animal—cows in the East, horses in the West—to pull the plow and till the land. Eventually came the tractor, and the animal was replaced by internal combustion engines to till that land. Other aspects of the agricultural process also witnessed similar developments, going from a dependence on nature for irrigation to the development of sophisticated means to bring water to the land. Such technologies have transformed the parched deserts to places where agriculture is routinely possible.

What is, however, important to note is the fact that each phase of the developmental process included the development of a tool. Technology was mobilized to devise the tool. Indeed, it is rarely the case that engineers and technologists start without a clear concept of what the tool would be and what it would be used for. To the designer of technology the paramount question is, "What will this tool do?" Even to a non-engineer, perhaps a child with a toy set made up of building blocks, it is rarely the case that a child will have no concrete answer to the question, "What have you made with the blocks?" The answer would describe it as something; rarely would the child say, "I do not know!" Makers of things often have a sense of the use of the thing they have made. Engineers and technologists are, of course, also interested in questions about efficiency and convenience, but it is usually the case that a thing is made to do something.

Doing something is, however, not a static construct. The "something" and the way it is done tend to change. Thus, another aspect of technology that is worthy of note is that developments in technology represent improvements in how well something is done—how well a tool does what it was meant to do. Technological innovation would never have happened without the desire to do things better. The fundamental human desire to make one's condition better calls for technological development, with the assumption that new technologies will improve the human condition in some fashion. This motivation is fundamental to technological change and is frequently the basis for many different motivators of technological change. Often new scientific inventions offer insights that lead to the development of new technologies, just as urgent demands in everyday life motivate the production of new technology to address those needs. Consider, for instance, the invention of plastic that led to an entire new set of industries where the availability of plastic allowed the mass production of things made from plastic. On the other hand, in a world threatened by terrorism, new tools have been developed to address the need to protect people from random attacks of violence. Independent of what drives the change there often is an assumption that the technological development is an indicator of advancement.

Given the emphasis on improvement and advancement, it is interesting to explore how the notion of "improvement" can be constructed in contradictory ways. In particular, not all improvements might be desirable. To go from the bow and arrow to chemical weapons certainly represents amazing leaps in the development of tools of massacre but arguably those are not necessarily desirable improvements. The story of the development of the first atomic weapon in the American deserts of New Mexico illustrated how efficiently it was possible to harness the power of the atom to bring about horrendous death and destruction. Indeed, the level of casualty that can be inflicted with the use of one atomic bomb could have required thousands upon thousands of soldiers with bows and arrows, and that too would not have been particularly efficient because the soldiers along with their victims would have been in significant danger. Not only was there mutual danger in hand to hand combat in the days of swords, maces, bows, and arrows, but also the killing was peculiarly personalized. Chopping off even a single head spills blood that gets on the body of the killer! However, the co-pilot of Enola Gay, the US B29 bomber that dropped the atomic bombs on Hiroshima killing nearly 118,000 people and destroying nearly 45,000 buildings, said, "Fifteen seconds after the flash [after the bomb exploded] there were two very distinct slaps and that was all the physical effects we felt". Very different from the blood spilled by a sword! The focus on development thus brings me to a critical component in the discussion of distance from technology—the way we feel technology and its consequences. It is important to focus on the idea of feel simply because our connection with technology is often based on the way in which we are able to manipulate the tool by interacting with the gadgets. Thus, there has been an amazing amount of attention paid to the idea of ergonomics where engineers try and work out the way in which a device can be made more "user-friendly" or even more physiologically pleasing to use.

In many ways, the difference between using bows and arrows to slaughter and using precision-guided missiles to kill illustrates the way in which the feel of technology changes with each level of improvement. The history of the development of the automobile provides some telling examples of the notion of "feel". Although it was agreed that the automobile provided significant improvements over the horse carriages, there were palpable problems with the operation of an automobile. Dirt roads led to the quagmire of mud in which automobiles were often stalled, the roads with potholes led to frequent failure of axles, and in the days of rack and pinion steering the driver literally had to fight the road in order to be able to drive the car, making the process of riding in an automobile an experience that sometimes did not feel well. At the same time, there was a connection between the driver and the car that was nearly visceral and the primitiveness of the technology kept the driver more aware of the road being driven on. Shock absorbers were neither popular nor efficient. Indeed, the following recounting of the history provides a sense of the way in which automobiles worked:

> On a summer day in 1904 a young man by the name of William Brush helped bring about the modem automobile suspension system. Driving his brother Alanson's Crestmobile, Brush was rolling along too fast for the unpaved roads of the day and went into a curve at 30 mph. The car's right front wheel skittered onto the dirt shoulder and whammed into a deep rut. Almost at once, the wheel started to shimmy violently. The undulations of the jarred right front elliptic leaf spring had sent shock waves across the solid I-beam axle to the left side of the vehicle. This set the entire front of the car to vibrating furiously. Brush was caught unawares and lost control. The car crashed through a barbed wire fence, hit a ditch and overturned in a cow pasture.[1]

This story not only illustrates the issue of technological improvements but also represents the fact that the technology was indeed very conspicuous. The shaking, the jarring, the vibrations, and the feel of the road (or lack thereof) made the driving process a challenge. Anyone who has driven a car without "power steering" knows well how a car "feels" on the road.[2] Indeed, in the days before power steering it was important to be able to feel the road to be able to drive.

The notion of feeling the technology to operate the technology has been true for numerous areas of human endeavor ranging from flying an aircraft to the practice of medicine. For instance, much like the older cars, airplanes started to use hydraulic controls only following World War II after which airplanes became too large to be controlled simply by feeling its movements and thus it was necessary to provide the pilot with additional help in controlling the aircraft. Prior to that, a pilot had to be physically strong to just pull the joystick and control the rudder since it required significant prowess to move these things to control the aircraft. This was certainly not very efficient, yet the pilot had to feel the plane to fly the plane.

Similarly in medicine the notion of "feeling" the patient was a part of the diagnosis process. To be sure, the term "palpation" refers to the medical practice of feeling a patient's body to look for telltale lumps and other abnormalities that could be signs of bigger problems. The quality of a doctor was often judged by the doctor's ability to diagnose problems by this process of understanding the patient and being able to evaluate the patient through a process of human examination without the need for many sophisticated tools. That trend has now increasingly given way to the tool-based practice of medicine, which no doubt is more efficient, but has distanced the doctor from the patient to the degree that the patient now needs to be "checked with tools" rather than felt.

Examples such as this abound in the development of technology with an essential common strain—there is an increasing distance between the work performed by the tool and the user of the tool. The driver of the modern automobile need not feel the road to drive, the pilot of a modern aircraft can fly it with feather touches, the soldier of today need not look the enemy in the eye to kill, and a doctor need not even see the patient to heal. What has remained unchanged is the fact that each of these moments in technological development has represented amazing improvements in the tool and what the tool can do. However, in the desire to produce better tools, the relation between the tool and its user has primarily been considered as an engineering challenge too with the key goal of making the tool easy to use. Ironically it is this ease of use that also leads to the process of alienation with its numerous consequences.

ALIENATION

The notion of alienation has been a focus of study from many different perspectives. For example, the approaches taken by political economist Karl Marx[3] and by the psychiatrist Sigmund Freud[4] have been some of the more well-known perspectives on the idea of alienation. In the works of Marx and Freud there was the common theme that alienation involved the distancing between two entities. Thus, Marx argued that the practice of capitalism produces a distance between the laborer and the product of his or her labor. Specifically, Marx was concerned about the way in which the laborer is separated from the profit that is gleaned from the work of the laborer. In an explicitly economic analysis, alienation for Marx was a key component of the development of a socialist political economy. He argued that a better economic system would be created if the wage earner became the owner of the means of production and is thus no longer distanced from whatever profit the work produces. The focus for Marx was on discovering a way to reduce the alienation between the efforts of the work of an individual and the product of that work. Even though many of Marx's analyses and conclusions remained worthy of debate, his work was able to point towards the phenomenon of alienation as a noticeable aspect of early industrial economic systems in Europe. To Marx, reducing the level of alienation was an important and urgent concern because of his conviction that once the alienation was reduced a new utopian and fair society could be produced.

Working in a time period similar to Marx, Freud, on the other hand, took a different approach to alienation because not only was Freud not interested in a political economic theory but also there was no great urgency in Freud's analysis on reducing alienation. For Freud, alienation was essentially the natural split between the conscious and the subconscious aspects of the human mind and from the psychoanalytic perspective this mode of alienation was a part of the evolutionary process of being human and there was no specific question of overcoming this alienation. To Freud, humans were expected to live with a certain degree of alienation which was internal to the human being and an essential part of life. The question of reducing the alienation would only arise when the extent of the alienation got so remarkable that the individual failed to operate within the accepted norms of a societal system. At those times, alienation was no longer internal but began to have an impact on the relation between the individual and the environment. However, even in such cases the alienation was internal to the human being and was not triggered by the environment, but there would be a need to reduce the alienation. For both Marx and Freud there was the concern about reducing alienation when the conditions became difficult and unbearable. While Marx and Freud have been the two key scholars who have historically been connected with the idea of alienation, others like Erich Fromm[5] and Emile Durkheim[6] have also used and developed notions of alienation to underscore the distance between the human being and society. In most cases the focus has been on identifying the factors that cause the alienation and then finding mechanisms for reducing the alienation to an acceptable level.

Eventually, the notion of alienation actually remains a very well-examined notion in psychology, philosophy, politics and related disciplines and in most cases the emphasis has been on the ways in which the human being is being distanced from events around him or her. In much of the discussions about alienation, thinkers have tried to find ways to reduce the extent of alienation. The desire to reduce the sense of distance between the individual and the surroundings, particularly when alienation is triggered by external forces, is motivated by the fact that the outcome of alienation can be fundamentally painful to the individual. To feel that one is distanced from the surrounding, or to feel unfamiliar and unacknowledged can be a debilitating experience. The sense of loss of control that can emanate from being disempowered has been the focus of discussions in politics and economy for a long time and attempts have been made to understand why alienation occurs and how it can be overcome. No wonder alienation has received so much attention because it is considered to be an unpleasant and abnormal condition because of the uncertainty and anxiety it can produce. Most of the scholars would argue that to be alienated is essentially an uncomfortable feeling.

While the current analysis draws from the traditional understanding of the notion of alienation, I use and expand on the idea of alienation to primarily refer to the idea of distancing. To me the notion of alienation is one that produces a distance between the human being and a specific phenomenon. There could be many different reasons for the production of the distance but my primary interest is in recognizing that there is a detachment. The distance can remain unrecognizable and thus unexplored unless an explicit attempt is made to understand the nature of the alienation. Thus in the analysis that follows in this book, I am interested in tracing the nature of alienation between people and the technologies that surround them.

Indeed, for the phenomenon at hand—technology—the nature of the alienation can be understood in terms of the relationship between the perception of technological sophistication and level of distancing. In most cases, the more sophisticated the individual thinks the technology is, the greater is the alienation of the individual from the technology. Within this relationship between technology and alienation the idea of sophistication is two-pronged. On one hand is the *measurable* sophistication of a tool going, for instance, from the primitive bow and arrow to the Kalashnikov, and on the other hand is the *perceived* sophistication of the technology, in terms of how the user thinks about the technology. The latter refers to what the individual thinks about a tool often with limited understanding of the tool. Both these aspects of sophistication play a part in the process of alienation but often operate in different ways since the loci of these two forms of sophistication are in different places—in the technology and in the individual. It can be argued that the perception of sophistication is partly based on the level of knowledge the individual has about a specific technology. A technology can appear sophisticated simply because the person using it does not know much about the technology and that ignorance creates the aura of heightened sophistication and increased alienation. Thus a law of technological alienation has to establish the relationship between three constructs: *(a)* the level of *actual* sophistication of the technology; *(b)* the level of *perceived* sophistication which is related to the level of information; and *(c) resulting* alienation from technology. Thus the law of technological alienation states: as technology gets more sophisticated the user perceives it as complicated and gets alienated from the technology.

Following from this law it is possible to find different levels of alienation with varying consequences based on the interplay between the actual and perceived levels of sophistication of the technological environment and the level of information about the technological environment. This environment is defined by the way in which technological systems constantly change with the primary goal being to alter the feel of technology. Most changes impact the way in which the user interacts with technology with respect to its feel, and alienation is related to the feel of technology simply because one gets distanced from something one cannot feel. Because the feel of "improved" technology is more "natural" there is a need to actively seek information about the technology to reduce the distance from the technological systems. Those who live in the complex technological environment and have sufficient information about the milieu would be less alienated than those who are uninformed about the surroundings and its sophistications. Yet, an important thing to note is the fact that the technological environment is itself a moving target for analysis. Different cultures offer different examples of technological environments and within the same culture the technological surroundings change over time. However, I would also argue that the law works in most technological settings at any moment in time. Thus the technologically advanced West offers a specific technological environment where specific levels of alienation can be traced using the law just as similar specific levels of alienation can be traced in the technological environment of rural developing nations. A farmer in a developing country who is unfamiliar with a diesel engine used for irrigation is as alienated as an office worker in the developed world to whom a personal computer (PC) is daunting. For the most part, however, this book deals with the new technologies related to the processing of large amounts of information.

To begin with, a fundamental level of alienation deals with the definition of technology itself. Given that tools are designed to do something, a very specific relationship between sophistication and alienation is established when the individual is faced with technology and is forced to ask the question, "What does this do?" At this level, the individual demonstrates that there is a fundamental lack of information about the use of a tool.

Another level of alienation refers to the way in which the individual is often driven by curiosity about the technology. Since technologies do things, a question that can appear important to the individual is, "How does it do what it does?" This question becomes particularly important when the technology is either perceived to do something well or when a tool fails to do what it was supposed to do.

The failure of technology is most noticeable when it ceases to do what it was supposed to do or ends up doing things it was not designed to do at all. Essentially, when the utility of the tool is compromised, the individual is often confronted with the question, "What needs to be done to make it do what it is supposed to?" Finding an answer to this question is critical to the user, because the response to this question can help to reduce the level of alienation from the tool.

The previous question begs the next one which is often critical to the way in which technological alienation operates—"Can *I* do what is necessary to make the technology do what it is supposed to?" It can be argued that those who can answer this question have been able to overcome several levels of alienation and have found a place where they can control the technological environment they live in. Others often remain hostages within an increasingly unfamiliar technological terrain.

I argue here that it is essential to probe the answers to these questions to understand the way in which technological alienation operates. These questions begin to point towards the various levels of alienation and their consequences. In the days of increasing complexity in the design and operation of tools, there is the anticipation that there will be some degree of alienation from the technology. It is no longer the expectation that the user of technology was sometimes also the maker of the tool with intimate knowledge of the tool. However, it could be expected that the degree of alienation can be reduced so that the consequences of alienation are attenuated and do not remain as profound as they often are. Reducing alienation is also not an easy task and would require the concerted efforts of entities whose motives and interests could well conflict with each other. However, I would argue that the law of technological alienation suggests a future in which the individual and the tools will enter into a relationship where the individual will remain at a disadvantage because he or she is alienated, and collectively the society of individuals will also be compromising itself because of large scale alienation from a technological environment where those "in the know" can control the destinies of those who are alienated.

2

The Cup Holder on My PC is Broken

A story that has circulated on the Internet and in techie parties describes a conversation that goes as follows:

Caller: "Hello, is this Tech Support?"

Tech: "Yes, it is. How may I help you?"

Caller: "The cup holder on my PC is broken and I am within my warranty period. How do I go about getting that fixed?"

Tech: "I'm sorry, but did you say a 'cup holder'?"

Caller: "Yes, it's attached to the front of my computer."

Tech: "Please excuse me if I seem a bit stumped; it's because I am. Did you receive this as part of a promotion, like at a trade show? How did you get this cup holder? Does it have any trademark on it?"

Caller: "It came with my computer, I don't know anything about a promotional. It just has '4X' on it."

At this point the Tech Rep had to mute the caller, because he couldn't stand it. The caller had been using the load drawer of the CD-ROM drive as a cup holder, and snapped it off the drive![7]

The CD drive of a computer could perhaps be mistaken for a cup holder. But what is more interesting to note is the creativity of the user who was unable to answer the question, "What does this pop out thing do?" and found a personal solution. Even though this story is most likely an urban legend it does demonstrate the concern over a level of user alienation which has been a part of technological change as illustrated in another similar story that predates the advent of computers:

> She kept on returning it back to the dealer, complaining that the engine was overheating, and was high on fuel consumption.
>
> This really baffled the dealer, as his mechanics repeatedly examined the car but could not find anything wrong with it.
>
> The young lady insisted that there was something wrong with the car. "It always happens when I drive it!" she informed the dealer.
>
> In desperation, the dealer asked the young lady to drive the car in his presence. So he sat in the passenger's seat and asked her to start the engine and take the car for a short drive.
>
> The young lady got the car keys out of her handbag, pulled the choke lever out to its full position, hanged her handbag on the choke lever, started the car and proceeded to drive it![8]

For those unfamiliar with older cars, the choke lever was a way to increase the flow of gasoline to the car engine to help start the vehicle on cold mornings. Typically, under normal driving conditions, the choke lever need not remain pulled. It is also interesting to note that this situation is impossible to picture now since the choke lever is obsolete because computers do what the traditional choke lever had to do. Stories such as these point towards the problems with answering the question, "What does this tool do?"

Users who are unable to answer this question can be considered to be experiencing technological alienation at a most basic level since they are confronted with a tool which could remain completely mysterious and somewhat magical to them. Thus, it is possible that some of the legends could be true because there could indeed be situations where the user simply has no idea what a tool is designed to do, particularly when faced with a relatively novel equipment and remains baffled by the tools that surround them, often finding inappropriate use for those tools.

The law of technology alienation focuses on the notion of being puzzled by technology. The simple fact is that until a user is able to reach a level of sophistication with a specific technology, the user remains alienated from the technology. At the core of the issue is the level of information that a user could have about a tool or task. The lack of information, however, need not be attributed necessarily to the user. It is not as if users are necessarily uninformed but it is more often the case that users are faced with specific technological conditions where it is almost impossible to assimilate the amount of information required to overcome all the different levels of alienation. Consequently, it is important to explore some of the key factors that place the user in this difficult position. In general, there are three interrelated reasons for the production of the first level of the alienation where the user is unable to even begin to comprehend what the purpose of a particular tool is. It is tempting to claim that the vast number of tools that surround a typical user is the main cause for alienation. That appears to be an "obvious" reason, but it is interesting to expand on the notion and consider some of the intricacies of the phenomenon. First, the large number of tools is increasingly of a special kind, where one tool is often designed to perform many different tasks. This is often called "convergence" where different tasks and tools are combined in one module. This leads to the second related issue of emergence of new tasks where the user is confronted with new tasks that are emerging and the user is expected to do those tasks. The combination of the convergence and the development of new tasks lead to the third phenomenon where old tools, and related tasks, simply disappear. Often, given sufficient time, users are able to overcome the different levels of alienation by learning what a gadget does, how it does it and even how to fix a tool when it is broken. However, as tools and tasks become old and are phased out, the user faces a new set of anxieties related to alienation. In this chapter, I explore these three issues and then draw the connections between these three phenomena and the first level of alienation where the user is unsure of what a tool is designed for. As suggested earlier, those who are experiencing the first level of alienation would most likely feel all the other levels of alienation. It is thus useful to examine how the first level of alienation is related to the three factors of convergence, emergence of new tasks and the disappearance of familiar tools.

ONE TOOL DOES ALL

At the time when I was working on this book, I remember a student interviewed me in preparation for a speech for his public speaking class for an "informative" speech on new technologies. The student insisted that he meet me in my office instead of doing the interview on the phone. When we finally met, the student also wanted to keep a record of the interview and pulled out his tiny digital camera. Not anticipating that I would be used as a visual prop for the speech I was somewhat taken aback, but the student proceeded to place the camera, after fiddling with it for a few seconds, on the table between us and began the interview. I was curious to know when he would take the picture but did not want to appear too eager, and I did not raise the question about the imminent picture taking but continued to answer the questions he had. At the end of the interview, the student fiddled with the camera again and put it back in his bag. This was certainly somewhat of a disappointment. It felt like that I was not to be his visual aid after all! I, of course, could not contain my curiosity any more and asked him whether he still meant to take a picture, and when he said that he had never intended to take a picture I had to ask him why he had taken out his digital camera and placed it on the table. He said that he recorded our conversation on the digital recorder that is built into the camera.

There are perhaps others who might also have experienced similar phenomenon where a tool that appears to be meant for one task actually does many different things, some of which might not be the obviously expected task for that tool. This phenomenon is often called "convergence" where different functionalities are lumped together in a single tool. The motivation behind the phenomenon of convergence is the quest for increased efficiency—an idea that has been at the core of technological development. Very often tools are designed and developed to perform a task in a more efficient manner. Indeed much of the history of technological innovation has been built around the quest of efficiency be it in the form of doing something faster, cleaner or cheaper.

The call for efficiency is, in turn, based on two other factors. First, the need for efficiency can often be motivated by the user of the technology where the people using the technology could ask that the tasks be done more efficiently. The user-centric desire for efficiency can well drive technological evolution and result in the production of convergent devices. Simultaneously, there could be a second force that is more technology centered. In this case, better technologies are developed because new scientific inventions demonstrate that new tools can be made. The user might have little to do with this process. Instead, development of devices and the convergence of tools can be purely technologically determined where the new tool appears because the new tool can be built. Both these driving forces often lead to the development of more efficient convergent tools. The consequence, however, could be alienation.

Around 1891, Karl Elsener decided to produce a light weight combination knife similar to the soldier's knife that would be user-friendly. The primary reason behind the production of the knife was to create employment in sparsely populated central Switzerland and the tool was legally registered in 1897. By 2002, nearly 34,000 of these knives were being manufactured and sold annually. This "multi-tool" is commonly called the "Swiss Army Knife" with nearly 100 different models with the largest one capable of performing nearly 33 different tasks. What is important to note, from the perspective of the law of technological alienation and its relationship to convergence, is that not many of the latter models are sold because they are large and somewhat bulky. The most popular ones are the smaller lightweight knives with fewer functions and easier operation.

In many ways, the Swiss Army Knife demonstrates some of the benefits and burdens of convergence. The fact that most popular among the Swiss Army Knives are the simple and small ones shows that when multiple tasks are built into a single tool, the user needs to become increasingly sophisticated to be able to discern the functions of the tool. The inability to understand the multiple functions creates the sense of alienation which ultimately leads to the point where the functionalities remain unused simply because the technology has become alien to the user. In other words, users shy away from the larger knives because they are unable to find a convincing answer to the question, "What does this do?" Yet, convergence was supposed to answer precisely this question by providing the user an ostensibly efficient multitasking tool that was supposed to be able to do all the things a user could need to do—from opening a bottle to flossing teeth as in the case of the upper-tier Swiss Army Knives. Yet, unless the user has overcome the first level of alienation it might be unclear that the same tool could be used for so many different tasks. Thus, the benefit of being able to use a convergent tool for so many different tasks is simply not met because of the alienation from the tool. Indeed it becomes a burden (often literally for the bulky Swiss Army Knife) to use a multi-tool because the user could often be mystified about the many tasks that a tool can potentially perform.

Yet, there is often minimal concern on the part of the technologists with respect to the design and manufacture of convergent tools. It appears as if the industries assume that the average users have always overcome the first level of alienation and thus are always excited to see the benefits of convergence. Often the concerns about the user's alienation become unimportant because the process of convergence is also motivated by the technological possibilities that were offered by advances in technology. Just as specific needs and demands can lead to the invention of multitasking tools, technological developments can also be the reason why such tools are invented. Consider, for instance, the way in which the radio reception technology has changed over time. In the beginning of the development of the radio technology, the receivers were large and bulky because their operation depended on the vacuum "tubes". These could be about two inches tall and an inch in diameter and a typical radio could need a dozen such tubes making the whole unit rather big. Radios were often like large screen TVs of the early twenty-first century and the radio receiver would take up significant space in whichever room it was kept. The development of the silicon-based transistor/semiconductor technology revolutionized the industry by making it possible to pack the functionality of a large radio set into the palm of one's hand in what was colloquially called the "transistor".

While the radio industry was moving in large strides towards miniaturization and portability, the sound recording technology was making its own moves to graduate from vinyl based recording to magnetic tape provided on bulky spools to eventually self-contained and sealed cassette tapes that were significantly smaller and much more convenient than spools of tapes. With the development of the transistor radio and the cassette player, the industry recognized an opportunity to converge functionalities—radio reception and sound recording, and the "two-in-one" was born because the technology made it possible. Whether there was a real need for the new tool would remain unclear since the two-in-one represented a more complex gadget that required relearning the way in which some basic tasks were to be performed. The two-in-one was thus born not necessarily out of a need on the part of the user to have a tool that could record radio broadcasts, but because it was now possible to make such a tool. The technology was available and the industry recognized the fact that once the tool was made it might be marketable. The two-in-one technology is particularly interesting because it stands in contrast with some other music technology that was quite popular in the period immediately before the two-in-one became well known. Companies such as Grundig were marketing large units often called music cabinets that contained a vacuum tube radio and perhaps a vinyl record player in a large housing. Most of these units could not record music; they could, like the two-in-one, play broadcast radio as well as recorded music. These units looked more like "furniture" than contemporary electronic units and were often marketed as to be considered as a part of the décor of a room. While the two-in-one and these larger units combined tasks, there is, however, a significant difference between the nature of convergence witnessed in the music cabinets of the 1950s and the emergence of the combined cassette and radio units of the 1970s. The furniture-like units did not represent the innovation of new technology but only represented creative "packaging" of existing technology. The development of the two-in-one represented a whole new technology that was invented and marketed. Thus the two-in-one represented a fundamental change in thinking about combining technologies into one unit. In the case of the music cabinets, there was a distinct separation between the radio and record player units and they often operated independent of each other. All that was necessary to learn was how each unit was operated but it was less important to know about the way in which the two units were integrated together.

The two-in-one, however, introduced the notion of integration requiring a level of sophistication on the part of the user which was qualitatively different from what was expected of the user prior to that. At the time of introduction of the two-in-one, there was little worry about the user's alienation from the technology and it was assumed that users would be able to overcome the first level of alienation perhaps because they were already used to the larger units that had the record player and radio built in together.

Yet, from the perspective of the user the first level of alienation as a result of convergence of listening and recording would be important. Before the advent of the two-in-one if there was an interest in recording sound from the radio, the most efficient method was to turn the radio on, place the tape recorder's microphone in front of the loudspeaker of the radio, and then play the record button(s) on the tape recorder. These were distinct steps that were separated from each other and were associated with each of the tools. In other words, there was no microphone in the radio, just as there was no station tuning dial in the tape recorder. There was also little confusion in answering the question, "What does this tool do?" The radio received broadcasts and the tape recorder recorded sound. Life was simple! There was little confusion about answering questions related to the functionality of the tool. However, once the two-in-one came into market, the customary knowledge about what a radio was supposed to do and what a tape recorder was supposed to do would not be sufficient to operate the tool. The level of sophistication required to understand the use of the tool went up. As a consequence, the tool was often not used to its full potential. In the case of the two-in-one, this often resulted in people using it either as a tape recorder or as a radio and perhaps not always as both. It was only after a period of time that the average user was able to overcome the first level of alienation to be able to begin to use the tool in the way it was intended. However, by then, other convergent audio tools had entered the market producing new concerns of alienation caused by the fact that one tool was doing too many things.

The law of technological alienation can be brought to bear on the process of convergence because the phenomenon of combining tasks leads to greater alienation simply because some of the functions are not used because of the alienation produced by convergence. It is important to recognize that the increased alienation is, however, a temporary condition. As the users are better able to understand all the different things a tool does, in other words, as they get sophisticated, the alienation decreases. Often the new found sophistication is a function of exposure to the tool or the development of a condition where the alienation becomes intolerable because it gets unproductive. Everett Rogers in his 1962 book, called *Diffusion of Innovations*, speaks of the notion of diffusion of innovations in terms of time it takes for specific ideas and developments to diffuse through society. He makes the point that it often takes some time before large portions of the population recognize the utility of a tool, and only when the utility is recognized and the sophistication is achieved is the new technology adopted in large scale.

Children provide a particularly good example of the way in which they are able to reduce their alienation from convergent tools by quickly answering the question about functionality. Thus, the advent of the "transformer" toys which were introduced in 1984 did not produce alienation; instead, the children embraced the toys and understood its functionality right away. This trend continues with children as they are able to quickly answer the questions regarding functionality of convergent tools since they have not been set into a "conventional" way of looking at tools. Convergence is thus a phenomenon that continues to introduce new tools simply by mixing and matching existing tools, many of which may be familiar to the user, but in their combination produce a new tool that remains alien until the user gains sophistication. The connection between development and convergence continues where many in the technology industries would argue that the new convergent tool is indeed an improvement over the earlier or different versions of similar tool and is thus worthy of attention and ownership. While the users are eventually able to learn to use the convergent technologies that do multiple things, there is a related challenge to understanding functionality that relates to the need for getting new things done altogether. This is a different phenomenon from connecting old functionalities in new tools. Instead, the process here involves doing new things with either old or new tools.

The new tasks could well be ones that an average person would never have dreamed of doing until technological innovations could make the tasks possible. What might have been in the realm of science fiction now suddenly becomes reality. However, the introduction of new functionalities brings with it the uncertainties related to the first level of alienation produced simply by the fact that the user remains unclear of the task itself.

NEW TASKS

In 2000, it was noted that 51 percent of American households had access to the Internet with nearly half of those households using electronic mail and nearly all of them using the World Wide Web. Such a report did not exist in 1980 when most US households did not have a "home computer". Exchanging messages by electronic mail was unknown to the average American householder in 1980, just as flying from one place to another was unimaginable to anyone in the 1680. Each of these activities can be thought of as "tasks" that we have invented for ourselves and have then constructed efficient tools to accomplish those tasks. Quite naturally these tools lead to the question, "What does this tool do?" The question is now prompted because not only is the tool novel but even the task is new. Even a simple tool might do a task that is mysterious to us and thus produce the sense of technological alienation. Unlike with convergence where the new tools lead to alienation, lack of familiarity with new everyday jobs can lead to alienation from the technology that performs those tasks.

Often the inception of the task is in itself a mystery and cause of alienation since it is not always clear whether the task was thought about first, or whether the technology was conceived of first. Somewhat similar to the commonplace "chicken and egg" question which has puzzled over whether the chicken produced the first egg, or the egg produced the first chicken,[9] the idea of alienation produced by new tasks is complicated by the fact that often the tasks are thought about only after the rudimentary tool is dreamt of, whereas there are also examples of situations where the need to do a task was so pressing that a tool had to be quickly built for the task. At the same time, new tasks would be constructed simply because there was technology that allowed the new tasks. The dilemma can be conceptualized around the airplane technology. The Wright brothers flew their airplane on the coast of North Carolina in America, and one of the brothers described the reason for making the airplane being their innate interest in flight sparked by the work of others such as Otto Lilienthal, the pioneer of glider flying. Thus, the tool tested in Kitty Hawk was built to not only demonstrate the workmanship that went into making the flying machine but also see if flight was possible. Many years later, in 2005, when the European conglomerate unveiled their super-jumbo jet called the A380, there was a well articulated need for the airplane since it could do a task that no other plane could do.

As Frederick W. Smith, the Chairman, President, and Chief Executive Officer of Federal Express, who was attending the A380 Reveal ceremony, said, "It [the A380] gives us a lot more cubic space, a lot more payload and a lot more range, but it also sits in almost the same parking dimension as our largest aircraft today and only utilizes one slot. That's a great advantage."[10] In this case, the motivation for the tool was to do a specific task. However, often the issue of the task–tool dilemma becomes irrelevant from the perspective of user alienation since what ends up happening is that the user remains unsure of what task a tool is supposed to do. It matters little if the tool came first or the task came first, since the user remains perplexed anyway. For many personal technologies, therefore, the tools and tasks get so intertwined that alienation arises from the fact the user is taken by surprise by the task and thus remains distanced from the tool. Conversely, those who are aware of the technologies and the tasks the technologies can perform are less alienated from the technologies. The key in this argument is the paradoxical condition that a tool might be very simple but the task it performs is so novel or unique that the technology and its functionality remain alien making a simple tool redundant only because it can do something we have never done before or felt could even be done.

Examples of this condition can be traced in the development of many tools. Scientific invention that motivates technological development is often geared towards the accomplishment of tasks that could not be done before. Sometimes those tasks could be so unusual that they appear to be improbable or the tasks could be so new that the purpose of the task itself could appear to be mysterious. Consider the simple task of trying to remember what appointments one might have a year later. The question that can certainly be asked is, "Why would it be important to know where I have to be 15 months later on a particular day and at a particular time?" In the conventional way of living our lives, this task could appear to be redundant for an average person. Thus, a tool that helps to accomplish this task, even if it is a simple tool, would be alien to the user because the significance of this task would remain unclear. Yet, there are simple tools, much like calculators, that boast the capability of keeping a 100-year calendar or store 5,000 phone numbers. Even a very popular person would probably not need to carry 5,000 phone numbers around all the time. However, this phenomenon has been made possible because of technological innovation where the combination of miniaturization and cost-effective manufacturing processes has made it possible to mass produce these tools and sell them at an affordable price. The user then needs to work out the purpose of the task that these tools can perform and only after that can the user reduce the alienation from the tool.

This phenomenon is evident in market trends where the consumption of tools goes up when the new tasks offered by the tools are better understood. The history of the Palm Pilot™ is an example of the way in which the consumer learnt the uses of the new technology. Often just called the "Palm", the tool is a compact, flat slate-like object, not much bigger than an average paper diary that has a screen on which the user can write with a pen. Whatever is written, a phone number, an appointment, or a note to oneself, is recorded electronically by the Palm and the user can recall that information when needed. When the first version of the tool was conceived of and launched as the "Zoomer" by Jeff Hawkins, the founder of the Palm Corporation, it became clear that there were not enough people willing to learn the new tasks the tool could do. This market knowledge helped Hawkins's group to rethink the potential tasks that the tool would be able to do and then redesign the tool with those tasks in mind which included things that became quite familiar soon after the tool was successfully launched in 1996. Yet, at the time of launching the tool, the average consumer, to whom Hawkins had targeted the tool, was confronted with a tool that was simple by design, but was able to do tasks that were new to the consumer such as recognizing the user's handwriting, thus setting the stage to do away with the keyboard which was a mainstay of the computing experience. Eventually this trend would result in the development and marketing of the tablet computer. Conditions such as this can produce the first level of alienation because the users were unsure of the specific things some parts of the tool would perform. Doing away with the conventional keyboard and replacing the act of typing to writing on the screen was an unusual enough task that could produce alienation.

The alienation that, however, follows the introduction of new tasks and the related tools is not restricted to the "average" user only. For instance, in a review of a newer version of the Palm Pilot introduced in 2000, a writer for a technological magazine said the following:

> I had been wondering why 3Com was cluttering its Palm line with so many different models and this one just didn't make sense to me: the IIIe was already out and seemed targeted for the low-end, so why bother with a Special Edition? Just because it had a clear case? Who cares about a clear case? I remember not understanding why people were so interested in the colored and clear Palm replacement cases that you could order; I mean, for me, the Palm's was attractive because of what it could do and its nicely shaped design ... who cared if I could see through to the internals?[11]

The tone of this review is suggestive of alienation simply because a "new" version of the tool was available. It was not clear to the author what task the innovation of the clear case would fulfill and, thus, even a trained adopter finds this innovation alienating. Alienation can thus well be the product of the fact that the new innovations and tasks appear superfluous and thus are either rejected or not used as often as they could be.

New tasks also emerge because there are technological and social forces at work that require new tasks to be learnt. The relationship between technology, social pressures, and consequent alienation can be explored around the popularity of the television in, for instance, American homes. While the TV is meant to provide a source of entertainment and information, the family dynamics in many homes often lead to using the television as a surrogate babysitter with the child placed before the television while parents can be busy doing things other than spending time with the child. This is not an uncommon use of the TV, but this utility of the TV brought with it the task of "policing" what a child would see on TV. This task of protecting the child from offensive media material was the product of the unique conditions in the developed and developing worlds where the combination of technological and social changes led to the development of the babysitting by television. No doubt, following the laws of alienation, the tool that could perform the task, however, remained alien to the user. To begin with, the idea of a computer control built into a television set was contemplated where the user would be able to somehow program the television to magically shut out any offensive material. However, the trajectory of the implementation of this technology demonstrated how new tasks and related technologies create a sense of alienation resulting in non-use of the technology. The controller, sometimes called the Violence-chip (V-chip) was introduced in Canada in 1995, but it was not until 1999 that the American media industry was beginning to think about adopting it and even then a news report on Cable News Network on July 1, 1999 made the important statement, "Earlier this month, advocacy groups and industry leaders helped two private organizations launch an education campaign to promote the use of V-chips and teach families how to use them". Thus, a user with the V-chip had to relearn how to use a television, which by 1999 had become a less alien technology at least from the point of view of answering the question, "What does this tool do?" The V-chip was re-alienating the TV technology because it was adding a new set of answers to the question of functionality by suggesting that the tool not only entertains but can actually be a reliable form of babysitting. Eventually, the V-chip technology never proved to be a great success. Rather, the media industry decided to rate its programs so that parents would know which programs are more likely to be offensive to children.

Often when new tasks are introduced and new tools are available to do the new everyday jobs, the users find themselves not only having to overcome the first level of alienation related to the new tools but also finding that the knowledge that was obtained about the use of the earlier tools to be redundant since the tool itself has become obsolete. Perhaps the task related to that obsolete tool has disappeared altogether. Thus a third phenomenon that is related to the first level of alienation deals with technological obsolescence.

TECHNOLOGICAL OBSOLESCENCE

There was a time when the answer to the question, "What does this gadget do?" was relatively stable. It might have taken a bit of time to arrive at the answer but once the first level of alienation was overcome, it was possible to stick with the answer and try and cross over the other levels of alienation. This was the age of "lifelong" technology where the manufacturing process assumed that the tool would last a person's entire life. This was a time when the dealer for the refrigerator would make the promise that a family could hope to keep the fridge in the family for the rest of their lives and usually these were minimal expectations that the fridge technology would not change too much over time. Equipment was built with the assumption that longevity was important and care was taken to ensure that the tool was manufactured well enough to withstand the test of time. However, the idea of technological obsolescence comes into play when the new assumption is that the tool would be replaced. As the word "obsolescence" suggests, the concept has to do with the way in which a gadget can simply become irrelevant and thus obsolete and the user is expected to discard the old gadget and acquire a new one. It is, however, important to ask two questions related to obsolescence. Is it obsolete because it does things that no longer need to be done? Or, is it obsolete because there are tools that evidently do the same task but only a little bit better? The answer to these two questions has a lot to do with the amount of alienation that the user has to experience because of the process of technologies going old.

If indeed a tool is obsolete because it does things that simply need not be done any more, then the issue of alienation disappears. The tool and the related tasks are gone and those users who were able to overcome the various levels of alienation can feel satisfied that they knew how that old technology used to work. In this case, the impact on alienation is minimal since the tool and the task simply disappear from everyday use and the fact that such a tool existed becomes a matter to be discussed in technology history classes. Often, such obsolescence is also controlled by the fact that the task itself was unnecessary or misguided where the tool disappeared because it became clear that task was not needed. A rather gory example of that process can be found in the annals of early days of medicine where there were elaborate gadgets to conduct the healing task of "blood letting". There is indeed an interesting history of specific tools, as described here:

> Bleeders used an impressive array of hardware. Their mainstay was the lancet, a small, sharp, two-edged knife. Wielding the lancet took quite a bit of skill; a false cut could slice a nerve or a tendon. To make the job easier a Viennese inventor produced a spring-loaded lancet, called a "Schnapper" in German or a phleam in English. It consisted of a case about two inches long with a spring-loaded blade emerging from the top. The bleeder would cock the blade, press the Schnapper against the skin and push a release, causing the blade to snap down and across. The Schnapper had the safety feature of not cutting beyond a certain depth.[12]

As this description shows, there was a significant amount of thought put into the development of the tool for phlebotomy as a therapeutic tool, but the tools became obsolete because the task was not necessary any more. To the user there was little loss and even if users were not fully familiar with the technology, any resulting alienation became irrelevant when blood-letting and its tools became obsolete. In a situation such as this, alienation becomes a moot point since the task and the tools have been removed from the fabric of everyday life.

However, obsolescence is also often driven by the factor that a new tool does the same task a little bit better. For instance, consider the case of the old wind-up record player with the steel "pin" that used to play shellac records rotating at 78 revolutions per minute (rpm). In the early part of the twenty-first century, it was possible to find these only in antique shops and immortalized in the dog and the gramophone logo of the music company called His Master's Voice (HMV). That technology became obsolete. In this case the obsolescence was motivated by the fact that "better" technologies came up that did the same task of playing back recorded music in a more efficient manner. In such situations the impact of obsolescence on the level of alienation could be less critical because the new tool did not do anything amazingly new but did it somewhat better.

A different kind of obsolescence results when the new tool not only does a task better but also promises to do new tasks. This is a situation where obsolescence, convergence, and aero tasks combine to produce a new tool. This has become particularly true in the digital age where the computer has continued to evolve rapidly. The rapid evolution is constantly alienating the user who laments that just as he overcame the sense of alienation with the computer, a new machine became available putting the user back to square one. Yet many users are unsure about how the new and improved machine is better in doing the tasks the user was familiar with. The matter can get particularly annoying when the old machine's obsolescence becomes painfully clear because it would simply be unable to do the tasks that the user had spent time learning.

This phenomenon is evident when looking back at the stages of the development of the PC. There was a day when most PCs (excluding the Apple line of computers) used to be based on a programming language called Disk Operating System, often abbreviated as DOS. Most users were able to overcome the first level of alienation with DOS by learning how to use DOS commands to do tasks such as copying files, erasing files, and running many DOS-based computing programs. Often, users were also able to write simple commands to be executed one after the other so that many tasks could be automated. A veritable industry developed on the production of the DOS-based programs which made life simple for the average user.

However, with the introduction of the mouse and the "desktop" with icons that could be "clicked" (often called the graphical user interface or GUI), the DOS-programs began to get obsolete. Much like the move from the music cabinets to the two-in-one, a major shift was underway with computing in the move from DOS to GUI. The user no longer needed to remember commands but could manipulate files on the computer desktop by moving the cursor over small pictures, or icons, of their files. The development of the GUI system led to the point where DOS did not seem as important. Yet, in the early days of the development of the popular GUI Windows operating system, computers using Windows would also be able to execute old DOS programs. This dual functionality continued for some time until a decision was made by the developers of Windows that DOS-based computer programs will be made obsolete and be phased out in future Windows development. By the time the XP version of Windows became popular it became impossible to run many DOS programs because the computer would not support these programs. Old tasks now needed to be done in a new way simply because the industry decided to make something old and unusable. The users who were familiar with DOS and had to change to Windows were now left with no choice but to give up their use of DOS programs. While some attempts are made on the part of the industry to accommodate the programs that have been made obsolete, there is often little desire on the part of the industry to support such "legacy" programs and tools since they are *meant* to be obsolete. Often this is a unilateral decision on the part of the industry where the user has little say and can only suffer new levels of alienation because something that they had become familiar with was taken away. Consider, for instance, what John C. Dvorak of *PC Magazine* said in 1995:

> There are probably 250 million or more machines running DOS, yet it's dead. But does it need to die just because Microsoft says so? How about letting the users control its destiny? I want to suggest that Microsoft, IBM, and Novell—individually or collectively—place the source code for DOS into the public domain so it can be further supported and improved by the users.

This never really happened and DOS simply died, again leaving many people alienated from technology just because it was decided that something would now be considered obsolete.

Obsolescence thus goes in tandem with the ideas of convergence and the discovery of new tasks. What it ends up producing are new levels of alienation that the user is left to deal with. Planning obsolescence is thus increasingly a part of the standard operating principles of companies that are in the business of developing new tools. With that in mind, the user can expect to be alienated multiple times as new tools are developed and the older ones disappear. The first level of alienation will thus remain an ongoing consequence of obsolescence which in turn is related to the process of convergence and the development of new tasks.

RESPONDING TO ALIENATION

There are thus several tendencies that are worthy of note with respect to the alienation that is caused by the inability to answer the question, "What does it do?" The process of convergence is leading to the availability of new tools whose functionality and task are not necessarily self-evident and thus the user remains alienated and fails to do all the different things the tools could do. We are often confronted with an attractive tool that we would like to be able to use but the very fact that we are unclear about what the tool can do alienates us. Often, the user might know some of the things the tool can do but is unclear of the entire range of functions the technology can perform. At the same time, there is the constant emergence of new tasks that need to be accomplished and the users could remain alienated from the tasks themselves and consequently get distanced from the tools that could accomplish the tasks that are unfamiliar. Alienation from the tools that perform the new tasks also makes the user wary of the new tasks simply because the tools that do the new tasks appear esoteric and beyond reach. Simultaneously, tools that were within reach can become old and go out of reach making obsolete the familiar answer to, "What can this do?" Yet, if the first level of alienation is overcome it is often possible to see that new ways of doing things and the related equipment make many activities simpler. Yet, the awareness that a tool could be very useful cannot be reached unless the first level of alienation is overcome.

To begin with, the law of technological alienation applies at a very fundamental level where the functionality of the technology remains unclear leading to alienation. This, however, also suggests that with increasing adoption of the tool and growing demand to perform a task, the users who could be experiencing the first level of alienation are often able to outgrow the condition by actively seeking answers to the question, "What does this tool do?" and then adopting the tool in everyday practice. Indeed, this is the level of alienation that users are often most aware of. Most people will say that they are aware of what they do not know. Although that sounds awkward, it is often the case that an averagely intelligent human being is able to acknowledge the fact that he or she does not know a set of things. When related to technology, this knowledge of one's limitations allows the user to realize that they are at the first level of alienation. That recognition also often tells a person that if they are able to overcome that first level of alienation then they would be able to live a better life by using the tools that they have around them. Thus, often, there is a motivation to overcome the first level of alienation.

However, there remains a constant struggle between the user and the technology at the first level of alienation because the phenomenon never appears to dissipate or disappear. As soon as one has mastered a specific tool or task there is the emergence of a new tool that appears to do an old task better or introduce new tasks in our lives. In a rapidly developing world, the new innovations come so quickly after one another that the user can genuinely feel the sense of not being able to keep up with the new tools and new tasks. It is not as if new tools have not been emerging all through the history of human civilization. But, so far, there has not been that much concern about technological alienation since most people eventually are able to overcome the first level of alienation before a new tool comes along, or the old one becomes obsolete. However, the pace of innovation has constantly accelerated. If one were to trace on a timeline the rate at which new tools have been introduced in society, it would demonstrate that the frequency has gone up with time. For example, the incandescent light bulb was introduced to the public around 1879 and it was nearly three years later, in 1882, that the first desk fan was introduced to make the world a cooler place. Two relatively similar technologies, one to light up our living spaces and the other to cool it, were introduced with a gap of nearly three years. Arguably, by the time the electric fan was in the market the users had overcome the first level of alienation with respect to the light bulb. However, in the early twenty-first century, products could be introduced within several months, even weeks, of each other as there is a frantic pace of innovation and a need to capture market shares before other companies can introduce competing tools that do the same task. As a result, however, the average user/consumer has to constantly ask the question, "What does this new tool do?"

The industry that introduces new tools and removes the old devices from the marketplace makes an implicit assumption that the user will enthusiastically adopt the new tool. Often there is significant effort on the part of the developers of the new machines and tools to help the consumer of the tool overcome the first level of alienation. The amazing amount of marketing of new devices can be viewed from the perspective of the laws of alienation and it is often clear that significant effort is made to inform the user of new tools. It is thus no surprise that new technologies are carefully "marketed" before they ever come to retailers. Quite naturally such publicity campaigns make much of the argument that the new tool or task would indeed immensely improve our quality of life and thus adopting the new tool and task is good for us.

Consider, for instance, the innovation and marketing of a personal music tool called the iPod™. Essentially, the tool is not much different from numerous other similar music players and composed of a digital music storage system and the circuitry to produce sound. The portable tape player and later the portable CD player all performed the same task. The iPod™ took the same tasks, but elevated them to a higher level of efficiency by offering the user the opportunity to store thousands of songs, organize the songs in specific 'play lists', and then package all of the technology in a user-friendly tiny device. However, the company that introduced the iPod also did not spare any efforts to hype the product to highlight the technological and cultural "coolness" of the tool to the extent that a commentator said the following about the earlier technologies of the portable CD and tape players, "Whenever I saw someone on the street with a Walkman or a Discman, I'd think, 'Oh, that is so last century.' I'm not alone, of course. Apple has sold millions of iPods since introducing the device three years ago."[13]

This comment demonstrates how well the product was able to "place" itself in relation to other tools that did the same task. The alienation that could be produced by the introduction of the new tool was overcome by carefully marketing the product. The iPod was particularly successful in marketing itself with an advertising budget in millions of dollars where the potential user was sold the idea of the new tool which promised to do the old task of playing personal portable music better. The success of the iPod is a good example of the way in which the alienation related to a specific tool can be significantly reduced if there is sufficient information about the tool as the tool is introduced.

The idea of marketing is also intimately related to education. The laws of technological alienation state that increasing knowledge reduces alienation. Thus at the first level of alienation if the user is given sufficient information about the gadget then there could be an automatic reduction of alienation. Thus it becomes imperative to focus on the education about the functionality of a tool to help the users overcome the natural alienation that is experienced when a new tool or task is confronted. The process of education therefore becomes the key to overcoming the first level of alienation. Interestingly, within the free market system there are two groups who are equally interested in ensuring that a certain level of education is provided so that the tool is used. Surely the user group would want to be educated, but it is also in the interest of the manufacturer of the tool to provide the information about the functionality of the new tool so that the tool is purchased and used. This is the role that advertising has traditionally played in selling technology and there appears to be an increasing interest in providing advertising that explicate the function of a tool very clearly.

Consider the ubiquitous Windows operating system. An average computer user would remember that the operating system went through numerous transformations from its early days. The Windows software started in the late 1980s and early 1990s as an offshoot of the DOS system and went through many versions among which the Windows 3x series of the 1990s were considered a milestone, followed by the Windows 9x series introduced in 1995 as Windows 95, and then a "new" version introduced in 1998 as Windows 98 to be followed by a series of other versions eventually culminating in the Windows XP version introduced in 2001.

In this history of nearly 20 decades, an interesting moment occurred in 1995 when Windows 95 was introduced. At this time, DOS was to disappear in the background and some new features were to be introduced to the consumer. Thus the question of "What does this do?" became particularly important when the 95 version was being introduced. Indeed the consumer was apprehensive about the possible alienation that could be produced by the new software and thus Microsoft Corporation was faced with the need to reduce this alienation while demonstrating that the product would do different and better things. The company thus embarked on one of the most expensive advertising campaigns known in history. Prior to the release of the computer program, a strategic marketing campaign was launched to create an immense hype for the program and to educate people about the program. This was achieved through traditional forms of advertising and by planting news stories about the product in popular media. Innovative ideas were utilized such as the use of the popular rock music group, Rolling Stones, to sing the theme song for Windows 95 which evoked the open-ended potential of the operating system and referred to the introduction of the "start" button of the Windows operating system in the song, "start me up". Indeed as was reported at that time, people lined up for hours outside computer stores to purchase their personal copy of the operating system, including people who did not own computers! The marketing campaign that cost Microsoft and its partners nearly a billion US dollars was thus incredibly successful.

The success of the marketing campaign for Windows 95 resulted in a large number of people frantically attempting to overcome the first level of alienation with respect to Windows, which was emerging the major name among all the competing operating systems. The user was left with little options as new computers were sold with the operating system already built into it and thus the alienation related to not knowing what the program did had to be quickly overcome in order to be able to use the computer which was becoming a mainstay of all facets of life. It is at these moments that the effect of obsolescence also becomes particularly important. In the period of 1995 and 1998, the Internet saw phenomenal growth and the Windows 95 system was already obsolete in some ways by 1998 since it did not offer robust tools for exploring the vast and emerging world of the Internet. Thus, the company introduced a new version of Windows in 1998 and labeled it Windows 98. The key selling logo for this system was, "Where do you want to go today?" This was a reference to the power of the Internet that would be harnessed by the Windows 98 operating system. While Microsoft was embarking on an elaborate marketing campaign to promote Windows 98, in the opinion of the industry reviewers, however, the Windows 98 was not considered to be a vast change as the advertising would have had you believe. Indeed, in the July 1998 issue of *PC World* magazine, Scott Spanbauer wrote, "If Windows 95 was a great leap forward, Win 98 is a series of baby steps. No single feature of this $90 (street price) upgrade screams 'buy me, and many improvements are available as free downloads or in recent Win 95 versions.'" Thus, from the perspective of the reviewer the answer to the question of, "What does it do?" was essentially that it was not much different from the product that was already out there and users were familiar with. Similar arguments were made by other reviewers such as Kristi Coale who said in June

1998, in *Wired Magazine*, "But for all the talk of integrating the once-disparate technologies, Microsoft's (MSFT) additions make Windows 98 little more than a shrink-wrapped service pack. And this leaves the top software company to answer one simple question: Why upgrade to Windows 98?"

The challenge for Microsoft was simple. It needed to be able to sell a "new" product that people would perceive to be sufficiently different from the old product but not so different that the laws of technological alienation would kick in and the sales of the product would be impacted. This is where the relations between obsolescence and alienation became acutely clear and part of Microsoft's response was to generate the sense of a "new" tool by combining different functionalities in the tool. Starting with Windows 95 and then solidifying with Windows 98, Microsoft converged the experience of using a computer and browsing the Web in one packet by combining its operating system and its Internet browser—Internet Explorer—in such a way that, as a Microsoft personnel said, "We will bind the shell to the Internet Explorer, so that running any other browser is a jolting experience."[14]

While this was mainly a response to the threat of losing market share to competing browsers, these strategies illustrate how the law of technological alienation needs to be kept in sight when new products are brought to the market. Whenever new tools and tasks are introduced it is likely that the user would ask questions such as, "What does this tool do—does it run the computer, or is used to browse the Web or both?". In the case of Microsoft, the company was very successful in meeting the challenge and through an expensive and creative advertising campaign it was able to re-orient the user of the product to have an adequate answer to the question, "What does this do?" before the product was available to the user. Indeed it is important to note that there was an intrinsic recognition of the challenges posed by the first law of technological alienation and that challenge was faced head-on in the advertising campaign. Thus the company was able to partially anticipate the initial level of alienation that users could feel and use the extensive marketing and publicity campaign that resulted in people eventually lining up outside retail stores to get their copy of the new software even though many in the software industry were skeptical of the value of the new product and users also learnt quickly that while the Windows 98 advertising got them enticed, the system did not really get to be completely operational until the release of Windows 98 Second Edition, which came nearly a year after the release of the Windows 98 version.

Not being able to answer a question about the use of a technology can become a particularly frustrating experience since we are increasingly surrounded by new technologies that seem to combine different kinds of functions into one. Along with combining functions, we are also in the constant process of discovering new tasks that we must do with all the new tools that engulf us. Finally, even as we are able to figure out what a gadget does, that particular tool disappears from the marketplace and a new one is introduced. These different factors certainly distance us from what we use and we often have to spend significant amount of time and effort to learn the answer to the question, "What does this thing do?" Thankfully, there are often sufficient resources to help us find the answer to the question. Even if the answer is not complete and exhaustive, it is often enough for us to be able to use the technology to a certain degree of efficiency. In other words, we might never know for sure what some of the settings and buttons on the digital camera do, but we are able to overcome the first level of alienation to know that it is a digital camera. To some, that knowledge could be satisfactory enough and no other question needs to be answered about the tool. I would, however, argue that knowing what the equipment does is only the first step towards reducing the distance between us and our tools, and it is important to recognize the other levels of alienation, even if we cannot overcome them all, to be clear about the ways in which we remain vulnerable because of our alienation.

3

Maybe My Monitor's Out of Ink

S imilar to the story about the coffee cup holder is the tale told by support personnel from a computer company. The technician answered a call where the caller's computer monitor was malfunctioning and the user did not see any color on the screen. The caller proceeded to make the assumption that the monitor, like the color printer, also needed ink and thus came to the conclusion that the monitor was out of ink since it did not have a good image or was showing only a black and white image. Whether this story, and many other like this, is true or not is an interesting subject of speculation. Like many other urban legends that circulate, it is quite possible that there might have never been an exact incidence such as this but something similar and related could have triggered the story and its circulation. What, however, remains important in this story, and numerous such stories circulating on the Internet, is the second level of alienation that users of technology often face in their inability to answer the question, "How does it do what it does?" In the case of the caller who claims that the computer monitor is out of ink, he or she feels that there is a plausible answer to the question of how the monitor technology works and is confident that the ink in the monitor makes it work. Thus, to this caller there is a mistaken presumption that he or she knows the answer to the question that is fundamental to the second level of alienation. Yet, not all users are so confident in their erroneous answers. Indeed in most cases the user simply has no answer to the question and is thus necessarily alienated from the technology because the user can find no reasonable answer to the question of how a specific technology works.

There are two key components of the second level of alienation that need to be considered. First, at the second level there is an assumption that the user has to some degree been able to overcome the first level of alienation. In spite of the sophistication of the technology it is assumed that the user who asks the question that is central to the second level of alienation has been able to answer the question of the function of a tool with some degree of sophistication. In other words, the user who is thinking about how something works has an adequate understanding what a tool does. Otherwise, the questions of *how* the tool does something might not even arise. Either through a process of using a technology often enough or through sufficient training on the use of technology the user who has "graduated" to the second level of alienation has been able to decipher most of the different things a tool is capable of doing.

A good example of this process is the way in which many people use the automobile. Beginning with driver's education for teenagers, users are given a fairly elaborate training in the use of the automobile with appropriate emphasis on safety of use. Typically a person driving a car has ample knowledge of what the technology is capable of doing and of the general application of the technology and its appropriate use. This might not be true for other technologies such as a video cassette recorder about which there have been sufficient number of tales of woe where users would not even be sure of the appropriate range of functions that the tool could provide. In that situation the users are still struggling with the first level of alienation and often have not developed sufficient information to even ask the question of the way in which a tool works.

Another component of the second level of alienation is the fact that not all users might be interested in asking questions related to the way in which a technology works. Often when users are able to use their tools efficiently the user is content with that and need not even ask the question of how something works. This is particularly so when the technology works well and is able to provide the functionality that it is supposed to offer. Thus if a car can take a driver from home to work, there is usually no urgency in trying to find out how the car works. Arguably if a user knows what the tool does and is able to use that tool well in their everyday life activities then they have passed beyond the first level of alienation and can simply stop there and need not think any further about the tool or technology. Indeed, the very idea of ubiquity of technology is built around the premise that the value of a technology can be judged on the basis of its transparency to the user. Thus, the technology of the contact lenses—a piece of "foreign" object we willingly apply to the eye—has become literally and figuratively transparent. With the increasing sophistication of the technology and within limited and prescribed use the technology has become ubiquitous because we do not notice its presence. For a technology to become ubiquitous it must be invisible to the user while the technology continues to provide the functionality the user demands from the technology. Once a user feels satisfied with the technology the user remains blissfully unaware of the level of alienation that the user is operating at since questions such as how the technology works is relegated off-stage and the technology simply takes centerstage as users continue to use it.

It is thus important to recognize why most users are disinclined to ask the question of how a technology works. As many commentators have pointed out, this lack of enthusiasm can be related to a well-founded fear that the technology is much too complicated and beyond the reach of the user. Consider for instance the way in which Debbie Farmer, the author of *Life in the Fast-Food Lane: Surviving the Chaos of Parenting*, describes her resistance to understanding the inner workings of the computer

> Oh, it's not like I can't understand modern technology or resist progress or anything like that. But, frankly, there are some things I don't want to hear about. I'm the type of person who likes having a little mystery in my life. I don't need to know why the lights turn on, what makes the car move or how the television works to be happy. I prefer to just go through my day thinking of it all as wondrous miracles taking place around.[15]

Yet it is this precise perspective that is shared by many other users that can cause extensive damage to the ability of the user to use the technology well. An interesting manifestation of the danger to accepting the "mystery" can actually be seen in the case of computers. Often computer products, particularly software, are released in the marketplace before they are "fully baked" and well tested. The desire to release the product in the marketplace to stay ahead of competition eventually leads to a need for the release of "patches" that the manufacturers have to constantly send out to improve the functionality of the tool that has been developed. Often the use of the patches for computer software is optional and the user can choose to ignore these updates. This is precisely where the problems begin for those users who are unsure about how the computer and its software work. Often, the alienated users simply do not know the importance of the patches and ignore them. Yet, these patches, because the way they work, usually provide much needed security measures to curb the spread of malevolent computer programs such as viruses. There is thus a cost to ignoring the updates and when the user is operating at the second level of alienation the cost could be hefty.

Experience with the universal Windows operating system illustrates this matter well. Ever since the release of the operating system's XP edition for the home and professional market, the company has offered regular updates to the system. Often these updates are no more than "fixes" that attempt to overcome internal shortcomings of the computer program. Often these weaknesses have been related to ways in which the computer program is susceptible to unscrupulous attacks by other computer programs such as viruses. What was, however, becoming clear to the authors of the operating system was that even those users who have gone past the first level of alienation were often unaware of the patches and were not using them appropriately simply because these users were operating at the second level of alienation and were unclear of the utility of the patches. The solution that Microsoft came up with was the "automatic update" where a computer connected to the Internet and operating a legal version of the Windows software would automatically receive an update from Microsoft and all the user would have to do is simply click on a few buttons and the magical update would be installed. This very process of making the update process transparent and easy produces the second level of alienation where the user gets increasingly uninterested in even asking the question about the utility of the update.

The lack of interest in how a technology works (as long as it works and there is a general understanding of the ways in which it can be used) opens up a vulnerability that can actually be devastating for the user and the tool. The propagation of viruses offers an interesting example of the way in which the second level of alienation takes place and the virus helps the author to make their destructive codes travel between interconnected computers. A virus is no more than a computer program. Unlike "good" computer programs, the virus provides the computer a set of instructions that are not appropriate for the computer and thus makes the computer do a set of things that are considered harmful. At the simplest level, a viral program could ask the computer to send a set of e-mails to the addresses listed in the computer's address book. Yet, the viral program is often dependant on some action on the part of the user of the computer for it to be able to do its evil deed. Most often, the user must be one who has overcome the first level of alienation and knows how to use it and uses it often since they find it a useful tool. Often, however, the user might lack a clear understanding of how an e-mail works—demonstrating the second level of alienation—thus helping propagate viruses. Notice that the frequency of virus attacks have gone up as more people are using e-mail. Interestingly, a user who is still unsure about what an e-mail is and does not use it is less likely to have the computer infected by a virus or propagate a virus. This is because the viral program often requires the user to open the e-mail program and open an attachment that has arrived with the e-mail. The process of opening the attachment invites the attached document to reside on the user's computer and thereafter become a "permanent resident" on the computer with the freedom to give computer instructions that the user never meant it to give. In other words, the lack of understanding of how an attachment to an e-mail works is one of the key reasons for the success of the viral programs. Indeed, the information technologists and support personnel often tacitly recognize the second level of alienation of its users. Witness, for instance, the instructions posted on the Web by the information advisors at the University of California at Berkeley:

> **Don't open e-mail attachments**. Many of the most recently detected worms depend on enticing you to open an infected file. These worms use "social engineering" tricks to get you to read the messages they send and, even more importantly, to get you to open their infected attachments.
>
> Be very, very careful with e-mail attachments, even those ostensibly coming from your coworkers and friends, as worms can easily forge the addresses in the "From" lines of messages.

Unless you have a specific reason to be expecting an attachment, *don't open or preview any e-mail attachments*. If there's any doubt, you can check it out by calling or e-mailing the person who purportedly sent you the attachment.[16]

These instructions acknowledge the second level of alienation suggesting that the user might not know how e-mail attachments work and is also probably unaware of the ways in which a virus works or propagates. The question that becomes interesting here now deals with identifying some of the reasons why users might experience the second level of alienation.

FACTORS THAT LEAD TO THE SECOND LEVEL OF ALIENATION

• INVISIBILITY •

It is important to begin to recognize that the key factor that leads to the second level of alienation is the increasing complexity of the new tools. The first component of the idea of complexity is the fact the complex tools remain hidden and are often invisible to the user.

The notion of invisibility is not to be confused with the idea of ubiquity that I have discussed earlier. While ubiquity refers to the way in which a technology becomes so familiar and "common" that we lose sight of its existence (except when the technology fails), the idea of invisibility refers to a planned move on the part of the technologists to make the technology disappear from sight, ostensibly to make it "easier" to use and make the users' experience a more pleasant one. The invisibility of the inner workings of the technology works off the assumption that users will know what the technology is to be used for but need not know how the technology works.

The automobile remains a particularly interesting illustration of this process. Opening the bonnet (or the hood for those who do not speak English!) of a car can produce a sense of awe as one is faced with a single chunk of interconnected metal which represents the motor of the car. This is very different from the engine of earlier cars that had recognizable parts such as the carburetor, the spark plugs, and other appendages that a user could learn about by picking up a book on how cars are built and how they work. The manufacturers of modern cars make the assumption that the user will not be opening the hood to do anything more than be mystified by a hunk of metal that makes up one of the most important components of the car. Gone are the days when people could actually recognize the different units and could perhaps even tinker enough with the car to be able to make a stalled car move. I remember the experience with a car in India. A common car on the Indian streets used to be called the Ambassador. Based on the 1948 British car, the Morris Oxford, the Ambassador presented a simple and accessible motor assembly that even an averagely intelligent youngster could understand and fix. Indeed, once when the Ambassador that I was driving stalled, all I needed was the help of a teenager from a local car mechanic's shop who with a few tubes, some wire and simple tools was able to get the oil pump of the car working again for me to drive it to a car repair shop for a more permanent repair. It is almost impossible to imagine such scenarios for the modern cars of the early twenty-first century.

The transformation in the automobile is not just a result of the technological innovations, but comes as a result of the way in which the user has changed. On the average, as illustrated in some of the anecdotes earlier, the user might simply not be interested in opening the hood and be perfectly content to live at the second level of alienation without worrying about how the car, or any other technology used by an individual, works. This is a curious condition, because it typically makes everyday life somewhat more comfortable since there is an assumption that the first level of alienation has been crossed and now the user can at least use the technology to its best potential, without having to worry about how the technology works. For the technology designers and manufacturers, there is no longer a need to make the technology itself accessible to the user as long as there are specific instructions on how to use the technology and the technology is designed in a fashion that a larger number of users will willingly use it. Indeed this is something that many would find to be the way in which technology ought to work. Dan Norman makes precisely this argument in his 1998 book, *The Invisible Computer*, where he carefully suggests that the best computer is one that is user-centered and has disappeared into invisibility while doing its work. In some ways Mr Norman's point of view can be considered to be proposing greater ubiquity. Yet, it is ubiquity that can result in the technology receding further out of sight of the user making the user increasingly unaware of what exactly makes a car work, for instance.

• INTERCONNECTION •

On the part of the designer and producer of technology, however, having the freedom of making the complex technology invisible to the user actually offers the opportunity to make the tools even more complicated and often intricately interconnected. Continuing with the example of the automobile, it is safe to claim that a car of the late twentieth century or early twenty-first century actually contains more computing power than the rocket that landed on the moon in the 1960s. This comes as little surprise since the lunar module had a relatively simple task to do for a far shorter duration than the average car. The module had to be guided by a very highly trained person to land approximately close to a predefined spot once and then take off and dock with another moving object only once. A car has to do a fair number of relatively complex tasks over and over again and needs to remain responsive to a variety of users with various levels of training. Thus, it almost seems normal that the modern car needs to be more complex than the lunar module to be able to perform its assigned tasks in the invisible fashion and remain extremely user-friendly. This leads to further complicating of the automobile technology where the automobile technology and the computer technology become closely integrated and a significant portion of the car's functions are controlled by computers. Thus opening the hood and approaching the car with a pair of pliers and a screwdriver might not be sufficient to either fix the car or begin to understand how the car works, but it is now necessary to approach the vehicle with a laptop computer and cables to understand the computer codes embedded in the computer of the car. One website on the computerization of cars reports that an average car today could have about 50 computer chips in it to do a variety of things from controlling how the engine operates to providing pleasing instrument displays for the user. Eventually, much of this complexity remains invisible to the driver.

The tendency to include computing in cars came as a technological solution to some of the problems created by the earlier automobile technology. Awareness and concern over the air pollution caused by cars led to the need for finding more efficient ways of running the automobile engine. This resulted in the use of computers to control the operations of the engine by introducing air temperature and pressure sensors and throttle position sensors that operated in the background, out of sight of the user, but helped to make the car more efficient. As these innovations were introduced in the automobile, it became clear that there were other places where the digital technology could play a role and need not remain hidden to the user. Indeed, making the user aware of the technology and training the user to use the technology could indeed make the car more attractive to the user. The automobile industry thus began to advertise its vehicles as complex machines that incorporate the traditional automobile engineering with emerging digital technology that would make the car-driving experience safe and fun. The car thus presents an interesting example of the way in which technological sophistication is related to the way in which different technologies become interconnected and in unison remain invisible to the user.

However, the car is not the only place where this is going on. Many other everyday technologies are rapidly becoming computerized and an interesting marriage is taking place between traditional technologies and emerging digital technologies. Examples can be drawn from a variety of everyday tools. Consider how modern refrigerators are becoming so sophisticated and computerized that some of these new coolers can actually sense the contents of the fridge and periodically inform the user what food might have gone bad since it was sitting inside the fridge past an expiry date. Cell phones can double up as cameras. Music players can be used to transport data from computer to computer and the television set can be used to check e-mail. Interconnected invisible technologies are becoming more of a norm than a novelty.

Be it the car, the refrigerator, a PC or the cell phone, the common theme is that the complex technology is invisible to the user. This invisibility causes the technology to recede into the background creating a sense of ubiquity. On the other hand, because the technology is invisible it stunts curiosity on the part of the user. The driver of the modern car often does not even know what questions to ask the auto repair mechanic since the alienation from the technology is so profound that one does not even know where to begin. This level of alienation essentially produces a sense of helplessness because the user of the technology often knows how to use the technology and also knows what the technology does but because the technology is so invisible the user remains completely unaware of how the technology does what it does.

While one component of complexity deals with the way in which technological processes become invisible, another component of this sense of complexity has to do with the way in which the tools are increasingly interconnected with each other and the user remains alienated because the interconnectedness of the systems remains a mystery. Yet the interaction between different tools is increasingly more important for the smooth functioning of many of the everyday gadgets and technical systems that surround us.

An interesting manifestation of this interaction between different technologies is the simple process of getting on the Internet to browse websites. Although there is no good count of number of websites that are available, it is the case that at the end of 1999, it was estimated that there were nearly 153 million people worldwide with access to the Internet. In most cases, these users were interested in obtaining information from the Internet using tools such as the Web, or the users were often using the Internet for communication activities such as e-mail.

The use of the Internet is, however, eventually the use of a relatively complicated system which is dependant on a variety of different technologies that must work together closely and efficiently so that the home user can seamlessly check e-mail. To begin with, one needs to have a computer for checking e-mail. An average user of the computer might already be somewhat alienated from this basic tool. However, having a computer is not sufficient; this computer needs to have in it either a way to connect to a phone cable or a more obscure thing called an "Ethernet cable". After the user is able to connect the computer to the outside world either with the use of a slow-speed phone connection or the higher speed Ethernet connections, the user needs to understand the process of getting an Internet subscription, an e-mail address, and then an appropriate computer program that will allow the accessing of the Internet and the e-mails. Thus there are several interconnected tools, systems, and conditions that must work just right for the user to be able to receive and send e-mail. All the different elements also need to work seamlessly with each other and remain as invisible to the user as possible so that the user does not have to feel either the first or second levels of alienation until the system quits working. This relationship between interconnection and invisibility often leads to the condition where the user is simply unable to answer the question, "How does e-mail work?" but has to be content with the belief that e-mail does indeed work.

Indeed, much of the design and marketing efforts on the part of computer manufacturers, software developers, and Internet designers has been to ensure that the user can remain relatively uninformed about the way in which the Internet works and how e-mail magically appears in the mailbox of the computer. All they have to attend to is making sure that for most part the interconnected pieces invisibly work together well so that the user need never ask the question of how they work together. The technologists gain a certain advantage in keeping this material obscure because it helps them avoid the need to educate the user about things that make the technology tick. By keeping the issues simple and invisible many of the problems related to answering difficult and unwanted questions disappear. An interesting trend in this direction can be found in the way in which computer manufacturers are increasingly doing away with the complex and often informative user manuals. If one were to buy a computer in the early 1990s, it was often the case that the computer would be shipped with an elaborate manual that would not only help the user understand how the computer works but would often have additional material about some software and programming that the curious user could learn about thus overcoming the second level of alienation. In the early 2000s that trend was replaced by providing a 'quick start' guide with the computer that the user could read in 30 seconds or less, follow the instructions and have the computer operating in no time. This accomplishes the task of receiving the e-mail but creates a huge alienation gap where the user of the Internet and e-mail would not even know where to begin asking the question about how the particular e-mail technology works because there are too many interconnected technologies that make this happen.

Most users of interconnected technologies end up operating with a sense of alienation as long as they can do what they want to do and understand what the tool can do for them. There is thus a level of ignorance that the users accept as normal and often feel comfortable with that level of alienation simply because there is a realization that the technologies are so connected with each other that it is perhaps beyond their capacity to understand all the components that make any particular task possible. The use of the Internet continues to offer further instances of the way in which the interconnections produce alienation. Consider the way in which the use of the Internet and the performance of many tasks such as shopping and money management are getting related. Increasingly many Web-based activities require the sharing of personal information. For instance, there are known concerns about the ways in which personal information can be misused with Internet-based shopping and online banking. However, the general user often remains completely alienated from the processes that are utilized to safeguard privacy and often assume that all is fine simply because of the lack of understanding of how the interconnected systems work. A study conducted in 2005 by the University of Pennsylvania demonstrated that nearly 75 percent of the users of the Internet simply act on faith and believe that if a website states a privacy policy then the Web merchant would not share personal information with third parties. Yet sharing and trading of personal information that is voluntarily divulged by users is a legitimate way in which information is shared even when there are stated privacy policies which are either ambiguous or too complex. Thus an online bank could well be selling contact information to telemarketers just because the two organizations are owned by the same conglomerate and thus the sharing is within the boundaries of the legal statement used as a privacy policy for the interconnected organizations. The point remains that because of not knowing how the policies work, and more importantly for not knowing where the information resides and the way in which it resides, users are often more trusting of the process than they ought to be. This is precisely the danger with the second level of alienation where the interconnected and complex tools become magical and people begin to forget to ask the question of how a tool does what it is supposed to do.

Just like with Internet commerce, where the notion of interconnectedness and invisibility goes beyond the concept of simple technologies connected together but gets into the realm of interconnections between organizations and corporate systems, the idea of a relationship between technological components needs to be understood in terms of the way in which different effects of technology can become associated with each other. A lack of understanding of the ways in which the consequences of the technology used are connected together also leads to the second level of alienation. This process of alienation, resulting from not understanding how the effects of technology are related to each other, can be seen with respect to medical and health care technologies. It is possible to claim that a medicine or a drug is in fact a tool that works in a complex and interconnected way to help remedy an ailment. Here the interconnectedness is no longer in terms of different digital and analog systems working together but operates at the realm of the body where the medicine can operate in many different ways having many different effects. Often such interconnectedness results in side effects and knowledge of how a drug works on the body can help the user better understand changes that are happening to the body because of the drug use.

Yet users of medicines often remain alienated from the process by which the medicine works in the body. There is often a sense of 'trust' that the medicine would work since the doctor, the specialist, has recommended it and the user does not feel the need to investigate the way in which a medicine could affect the body in the short and long term. This is not to suggest that all medicine users suddenly need to become specialists in health care, but the fact remains that there is an alienation from the way in which drugs work on the body that can lead to misuse and abuse of medicine. A good example comes from the way in which a common cold is often treated. Given that an average adult would experience the discomfort related to a common cold nearly three times a year, this ailment remains one of the most irritating diseases in humans. Till now there is no real treatment for the common cold and the best that is there are palliatives that ease the symptoms related to a cold without being able to remove the cause of the cold—a virus that comes in numerous different forms. The result of treating the symptoms is ultimately that the patient could become weak from the continued use of strong medicines that do not go to the cause of the problem but only provide temporary relief from the symptoms. To an average user, the questions that could be really important are how the popular medicines that are used for treating common cold work, and what other effects such medicines can have on the body. Yet, this is something that often remains unexplored and the user simply follows the trend of using specific medicines when certain symptoms are observed. This alienation can take on a particularly dangerous manifestation when the user actually ends up abusing the drug since there is a lack of knowledge about how the medicine does what it does and the user is only able to feel the outcome of the drug's work.

The dependence on the outcome has been one of the core reasons for the abuse of medicines. In a story published in July 2005 by Mary Pat Flaherty of the *Washington Post* she reports that nearly 2.3 million teenagers in USA use common medicines, such as painkillers, to get "high" and there are organized parties and gatherings where medicines are used as the intoxicant of choice. While use of intoxicants has been an age-old tradition among the youth, what is interesting in this trend is that it has come about because of experience based learning where the users have found that a medicine that was given to them to treat a particular symptom has ended up creating a feeling that could be habit forming. While teenagers might not be interested in reducing the alienation with respect to how the specific medicine works, it remains the case that increased societal awareness of the mechanism in which a drug works can help to better understand the possible use and abuse of drugs.

Indeed, this alienation from the interconnected way in which drugs affect the body is visible in great segments of society including among those who are supposed to be the specialists. In an August 2003 story, the National Alliance for Mentally Ill reported that there was some confusion about the relationship between prescription antidepressant medication and higher incidence of teen suicides among the users of the medicines. Of particular note was the story of Michelle Van Syckel who was prescribed a specific psychiatric drug and eventfully exhibited severe suicidal tendencies. This case took on importance and there was significant research conducted to understand the interconnection between a specific drug and several health issues. The case went on to demonstrate two important aspects of the science of medicine. On one hand there was evidence to suggest that greater amount of scientific research was required to understand the interconnections, and it was also clear that the general users of specialized medicines were quite in the dark about the basics of how complex and interrelated were the effects of medicines on the human body and mind. It is the second aspect that becomes particularly important since it demonstrates the level of alienation from medical technologies. Indeed, medicine has become dependant on different forms of technology in such a way that it is virtually impossible for the average person to understand how most of the medical technologies work. However, this inability to understand the technology and the lack of cooperation on the part of the experts create alienation where the users of many different kinds of technologies are simply unable to answer the question, "How does this work?"

While there are many interconnections between the technologies that surround us, a natural outcome of the expansion in the variety of tools—from medicines to gadgets—is also the fact that we are often inundated with technologies that have grown at an exponential rate. Technologies are not only related to each other but also there is simply too much of them around us that makes it often increasingly difficult to answer the question of how a specific set of technologies work. This adds to the second level of alienation moving the user further away from the tools that are around.

• PROLIFERATION •

Alienation because of the expansion of the number of tools around an average person can be traced in situations where people need to turn to expert help for using some of the basic tools of modern life. An example of the expansion of tools around us can be seen when trying to catalogue the numerous tools that are often used to do a mundane task such as keeping in touch with friends, family and business associates. In the simpler days before the digitization of most communication tasks, much of the exchange was done either with the telephone or through writing letters. Once it was possible to transform information into bits and bytes it was possible to find different ways of sending and receiving information. A quick review of the popular tools for these tasks could include the traditional phone tethered to a phone cable that comes into a home, multiple digital cell phones, pagers, multiple e-mail accounts, instant messaging using the computer, teleconferencing using video linkages and other emerging tools such as the personal digital assistant that can serve as a communication tool. This explosion of tools is particularly visible in the corporate world, specifically in the realm of the business traveler. Gone are the days of traveling light; now, a typical business traveler might carry a laptop computer, one or more cell phones, a personal digital assistant, perhaps a portable media player, different kinds of chargers, batteries, and headphones. While this creates problems in airport securities, it also creates a sense of alienation from the technologies unless there is a good understanding of what each piece of equipment does and how they are related to each other. Often the user is unaware of the way in which the units can be "connected" together and which of the tools become redundant because another tool does the same thing.

Alienation results from the fact that users are overloaded with the tools and they are unable to effectively answer the question about how each tool operates, and the manufacturer of the tools are not always forthcoming about this information. Take the example of the increasingly popular digital media player. By 2005, there were several companies making many different forms of digital music players. They worked in one of the two major ways, either these machines had a "hard drive" much like the one in a computer or they worked with little memory cards that could be inserted in slots in the music player. The difference between these technologies was significant because the ones with the hard drives often had the capacity to store a much larger amount of information than the ones with the cards. Consequently, part of the hard drive could be used to store work files and data which was often stored by users on separate stand-alone hard drives that could not play music. Essentially, there was often duplication of gadgets because it was not always clear that one tool could indeed do two or more tasks and thus one of the tools could be eliminated. No doubt, that kind of information has significant economic consequences since the un-alienated user could be saving money by being able to answer the "how does this work" question. Unfortunately, the plethora of gadgets make it increasingly difficult to answer that question and as a consequence people often purchase things that they simply might not need because they already have a different tool which could do the same task.

Much like information overload, where people are unable to process the explosion of information around them, the increasing amount of tools is leading to a gadget overload where the users are becoming progressively distant from the tools since it is impossible to keep up with the growth. This is further accentuated by the fact that these tools are often incompatible with each other and the alienated user can find himself in situations where the lack of knowledge of how the tool works can become so debilitating that the user's ability to work and be productive is radically reduced. The cell phone provides an interesting situation where the alienation related to the "how does it work" can become peculiarly troublesome. In general, most people have now become reasonably accustomed to what the cell phone is supposed to do and the preliminary level of alienation has been overcome. In the United States, for instance, at the current rate of adoption, nearly 76 percent of the people had cell phones in 2009. This large number of people are often remain unaware of some of the basics of how the tool operates. Consider for instance a series of exchanges on a bulletin board provided by CNET—a leading Internet based resource on new technologies—where the following exchange happens:

> What is the difference between Code Division Multiple Access (CDMA) and Global System for Mobile Communications (GSM)? I recently switched from AT&T to Verizon for billing and coverage issues. I was told that there is no difference between the two but I do not believe it. Any help anyone can provide would be greatly appreciated.
>
> In advance thanks for your time and help.
>
> Posted by: Blazedude - 02/12/2004 9:20 PM
>
> **Re: CDMA vs. GSM**
>
> If implemented properly, the end user will not know the difference.

What differences are you finding?
Posted by: R. Proffitt

Re: Re: CDMA vs. GSM
No real difference, just better coverage area because of type of phone. I guess what I am trying to find out, is one better or worse than the other and if there are any differences what are they.
Thanks.
Posted by: Blazedude (see profile) - 02/13/2004 8:58 PM
In reply to: Re: CDMA vs. GSM by R. Proffitt

This exchange continues with numerous other people discussing the various markets where the two forms of cell phone technologies—CDMA and GSM—are discussed but only one person among nearly 100 responses is able to point out the key difference in how these two forms of cell phones work in terms of the technology they use and also point to the fact that the GSM technology is available globally whereas the CDMA technology is available only in a handful of countries such as the USA, South Korea, Japan, and India. As a consequence, a person from India who carries a CDMA phone outside of the country will most likely not be able to use it in most parts of the world. Those who remain alienated at the level of how cell phones work could thus find themselves in an unfortunate position where the trusted cell phone does not work abroad. This situation comes about because there is a plethora of devices and technologists are still unsure about how to make them all compatible with each other so that the basic technologies are standardized. If indeed there was some standardization then being able to overcome the second level of alienation with one form of technology could help ensure that the user will know how other similar technologies work. Given that there is no tendency to contain the explosion of gadgets, the level of technological alienation caused by not knowing how a gadget works could be partially reduced when technological standardization comes to a point where the user does not have to learn about the way in which different tools work but can learn how one or fewer tools work and be able to overcome the alienation related to that class of tools.

The expansion in the number of tools and the proliferation of similar gadgets has been not only the result of corporate creativity but also fueled by the un-alienated users who because of their lack of understanding of how tools work often demand redundant gadgets. Eventually it can become a cultural and societal imperative that users must have *all* the different tools in spite of the redundancies. Perhaps if users were less alienated then such a tendency would be avoided and the users would have a better sense of how fewer tools can be made to work together to perform the desired functions. It is possible to notice this trend within some subcultures where the degree of alienation is lower because the average user has taken the trouble to overcome the first and second levels of alienation. In Japan, for example, the cell phone is not only used as a device to speak to another person but also serves as a mini-telegraph machine where users often are able to send short "text messages" to other cell phones and thus have a second line of communication beyond the spoken word. On the other hand the use of text messaging between cell phones is relatively rare in the United States. Interestingly, however, the capability is equally available in Japan as is in the US and the difference in level of use can well be attributed to the fact that the users in the US are alienated from this particular function of the cell phone and might not even know how to use the function let alone knowing how the function works. Indeed this is reflected in the 2001 article where the writer says:

> "I love you", in the newest language of today's lovebirds, is spelled 444 555 666 888 33 9 666 88. For those slightly less smitten, it's 99 666 88 77 33 222 88 8 33. That means "You're cute".

> Lost? Well, so is most of America. Those are the numbers you have to punch in on your cell phone if you want to use the

newest toy of the gadgerati, the wireless service called SMS. SMS, which stands for "short messaging system", is the high-tech equivalent of passing notes in class, letting cell phone users exchange text messages of fewer than five words.

This simple description demonstrates that there is a need for a certain degree of sophisticated knowledge about the tools in order to be able to use the multitude of tools to their full potential and to answer the question of how the tools do certain things. Of course, as we are surrounded by an increasing number of gadgets it becomes more difficult to answer the question about how a particular technology works and people have to remain in a state of alienation where most have to make do with the fact that they might not be able to fully answer the question about how something works but will have to accept that it does do a certain set of things without fully understanding the full potential of the tool.

• STEALTH •

The issue of alienation based on a lack of understanding of how something works actually gets more interesting when one looks at technologies that surround and influence us, but we remain completely unaware of the presence of the technology because the technology is virtually stealthy and secret. This condition remains another factor producing the level of alienation where the typical person is unaware of the existence of the technology and thus does not even know that the question of how the technology works could be asked. This condition is well illustrated in the use of surveillance cameras in various business establishments. It is not unusual to walk into stores, restaurants, hospitals, and many different kinds of businesses and not see the ubiquitous black or silver dome or sphere on the roof. Most of the times, these are containers for cameras that are watching the people in the store. The need to use the dome arose from the fact that they were more aesthetically pleasing than bare cameras, and it is impossible to tell which way the camera is facing at any time and the would-be shoplifters might be a little more cautious about their activities. The interesting thing is that the average person would soon forget the presence of these cameras and go about their business without even realizing that they are constantly being stealthily photographed and these pictures would be available to the security personnel of the establishment for a length of time. The alienation from this technology often results from the fact that the average law-abiding person need not worry about the presence of the technology and a shoplifter is deterred from a felonious activity because the person is unsure if they are being observed at that very moment. The technology, therefore, functions well and does what it does because people are unclear of how it performs its functions. The very presence of the black dome is sufficient to deter unlawful activity without the person ever understanding how the technology can actually do what it is supposed to do. This level of alienation is well understood by some companies that now sell dummy domes that are simply plastic domes or spheres which look like casings for surveillance cameras but are nothing more than empty shells that can be placed in strategic locations in a store to simply deter any unwanted activity. One can buy these things at local hardware, electrical and electronics stores and can install them with the use of simple household tools. The deterrence is based on the assumption that the person would have no idea if the dome is empty or not and the very presence of the dome would lead to deterrence because if an unwanted activity were to happen in the presence of such a dummy dome the owner of the establishment would have no way to record it or prove it!

Similar technologies surround most of us but because we do not see them in our everyday lives we feel no need to overcome our levels of alienation with respect to those technologies. Indeed these technologies are often so sophisticated that it seems beyond the capability of the average person to overcome the levels of alienation. Consider several technologies that surround us from lifesaving tools in Emergency Rooms to electronic databases that keep track of specific grocery purchasing habits that one has. The latter is an interesting example of a situation where vastly sophisticated technologies are at work in the background keeping a close record of an individual's activities yet the typical user remains alienated from the way in which the technologies work together to produce a condition such as the following as reported by Kelley Beaucar Vlahos in 2001:

> Chuck Jones, a spokesman for ChoicePoint, a data maintenance service that boasts 14 billion public records in its databases and information on 220 million customers, including credit bureau documents and buyer demographics, would not confirm whether his company shares marketing databases with the government.[17]

In fact these databases can have many different uses from the mundane ones where the user of a store loyalty card would receive targeted coupons when checking out of the grocery store to a more specific use where the grocery records could be used to track terrorists. As Hiawatha Bray of the *Boston Globe* reported in 2005:

> When you swipe one of those discount cards at the supermarket, you're letting the retailer make a record of everything you buy. Thus the store develops a profile of its customers' tastes and buying habits. Mining this data can reveal patterns that would otherwise go unnoticed.
>
> For instance, purchases of bottled water may increase whenever there's a sale on sirloin steak. Data mining uncovers thousands of these nearly invisible correlations, and marketing wizards use the results to maximize the store's profits.
>
> But data mining can also be used to spot interesting patterns in other kinds of data. Just by crunching credit card numbers, you could find out that there's some guy in Chicago who's been

buying an awful lot of fertilizer—the kind that can be turned into truck bombs. Or someone in New York who does a lot of travel to exotic foreign locales, and who also signs up for courses on how to fly jumbo jets.[18]

What is particularly interesting to note here is that the level of alienation from how the technology of data mining works is so profound for the average user that they remain completely unaware of the amount of information they are giving up and how that information could be used. But, for those who are un-alienated and are more aware of the process at work it becomes peculiarly easy to "protect" themselves from such invisible technologies. I will get into a discussion of this phenomenon later in this book.

There are, however, some technologies from which a user might not be able to protect themselves. Consider the way in which the satellite cameras work. When teaching a class on technology I often use an example that is sure to surprise students. I pick a student at random and ask him for the student's home address. This is information that is also readily available on the university computer's student directory and thus students are often willing to disclose their home addresses. I then pull up the website for the United States Census and in minutes I am able to show the class the details of where the student is from, sometimes with an aerial shot of the home. This is a technology that literally hangs over us, as numerous satellites are constantly taking pictures of the world with amazing levels of accuracy and we are often completely unaware of facts such as anyone with the access to the Internet and information about the home address of a person can get an accurate topographical map of the location of one's home. These technologies thus produce a special condition of alienation where we are simply unaware of the existence of the technology and how it works, but we are often subject to what the technology can do for and with us. In many cases, the consequence of the existence of such unnoticed technology is relatively benign but by not knowing the existence of the technology we remain alienated from the potential ways in which the technology could be deployed. Lack of understanding of how the technology works can eventually make it particularly difficult to work with the technology when it is deployed as was demonstrated in fiction in the 1998 Hollywood movie called *Enemy of the State* starring Gene Hackman and Will Smith, which shows how a particular individual can be carefully tracked with numerous alien and invisible technologies. The story was centered on a lawyer who is constantly running away from a series of surveillance systems as he tries to bring to light a series of criminal activities of people in the government. In summary, there results an alienation from some technologies because we often are unable to fathom how the technology works, simply because we might be aware that the technology exists and constantly has an effect on our lives.

SECOND LEVEL OF ALIENATION

In conclusion, several issues are worthy of note. The fact that we are often unaware of what a particular technology does results in a sense of alienation where the user is baffled when faced with a new tool or gadget. Typically, however, users are able to learn the purpose of a tool and are able to use it with a fairly high degree of efficiency. The ability to use the tool also often lulls the user into a state of confidence where the ability to use the tool is considered to be sufficient knowledge about the tool. Indeed, this is precisely where the larger industry of making and selling tools wants the user to be and often leaves the question of how a tool does what it does unanswered. So, there remains a certain sense of mystery and perhaps awe about the way in which a tool works.

Yet, this condition of being able to merely use the tool still leaves a significant component of the tool unknown to the user—the issue of how a tool does what it does. The user continues to remain alienated about this aspect of the tool. It is not because an average user is passive and lacking in curiosity, but the user often does not even know that it helps to use a tool if there is a greater and clearer understanding of how a particular tool works. This need not entail learning very complex, technical or technological information but asking (and receiving) enough information so that users would not be so alienated from a tool to perhaps assume that there are hidden ink cartridges in computer monitors or assume that over-the-counter cold medicines will actually "cure" the cold by "killing" the virus. It is this second level of alienation that establishes a relationship between the maker of a tool and its user where the user is expected to purchase and use things that remain a complete mystery to the user.

It can be argued that this mystery makes for a simpler life where the average user is not burdened with information about how every tool around him or her works. One could perhaps make a grudging argument that all users would not even be able to fully grasp even the rudimentary details of how specific tools work and need not be bothered by such details. This condition works well as long as the tool works the way it is supposed to. The matter changes when the tool quits doing what it is supposed to do, that is, when the tool breaks. At that critical moment when a digital camera quits working halfway through a vacation is when the question of how it did what it was doing suddenly becomes very critical. The user could be in a situation where there is no support to immediately seek assistance to get an alternative tool and the user has to come up with some solution to regain a critical functionality the tool was performing. The example of a digital camera provides a unique condition where many a tourist has found themselves "stranded" because their precious camera simply quits working and there is no easy way to capture the memorable moments of a family vacation. It is thus not surprising to see, at least in America, a growing number of shops where "disposable" cameras are sold at a cheap price precisely to address the situations where the alienated user needs to get a task done but the tool fails at the critical moment. Knowing how the tool works, and thus overcoming the second level of alienation can at least help the user to know what exactly is "broken" with the tool. Identifying the cause of a tool's failure is often directly related to successfully answering the question, "How does it do what it does?"

This condition of technological failure indeed opens up yet another area of technological alienation where the user needs to grapple with the question, "How could a tool be fixed when it is broken?" Overcoming the second level of alienation with understanding of how a gadget works still keeps some technologies alien because the user might still not know how to make a failed technology work and it is useful to explore some of the issues related to the level of alienation where the user has to grapple with the question of fixing broken tools.

4

Computer Problems?
Don't Go Nuts

*O*ne of the most frustrating moments while using a computer is when it simply does not do what it is supposed to do. Most computer users are familiar with the unpleasant feeling that follows a warning message that says, in cryptic terms, that you have lost the results of hours of computer work. A question that immediately comes to mind is about repairing the machine. The user of the machine faces a situation where the two levels of alienation have been overcome, and the user has a sense of what the tool does and generally how the tool works and the user has to face the challenge of fixing a broken tool. This has been true from the dawn of technology when human beings became tool-using beings. The fact that tools are made to perform a specific task makes it very likely that the task would not be performed if the tool ceases to work. At that moment, the user faces a level of alienation where the user must be able to answer the question, "Who can fix the tool?" There are several aspects to answering the question, but the level of alienation that the user must overcome first is recognizing that the tool is indeed not working in the way it is supposed to and thus the tool needs to be fixed. Sometimes that is quite obvious and the user knows that the tool has quit working—when a computer stops responding to key strokes. At other times, however, the malfunction might not be very self-evident.

IS IT REALLY BROKEN?

Users who remain alienated at the first and second levels might never reach the third level of alienation because they might not even realize that the tool is not doing what it is supposed to do. For instance, a person using an automatic toaster might get so used to burnt toasts that the user does not realize that a malfunction in the toaster is leading to the bad toasts. The desire to overcome the third level of alienation only arises when the user has a good sense of what a tool is supposed to do and how the tool actually performs its tasks. In the case of the person with a bad toaster, this would require some knowledge of how the toaster timer works. At that point the user is able to recognize that the tool is not doing what it is supposed to do in the way it is supposed to do it.

One modern gadget that has come to attention because the user is too alienated to realize that the tool is malfunctioning is the Global Positioning System (GPS). The GPS technology relies on satellite information beamed to tiny receivers that allow a person to know exactly where the person is with respect to latitude and longitude. Many cell phones such as the iPhone and some BlackBerry models have the GPS receiver built into the phone allowing the phone to stay connected to satellites in addition to the phone network. The GPS system also relies on the availability of updated maps that would use the satellite information to show the user exactly where the person is on a map, and in the case of advanced GPS tools, the user is actually instructed by the system to go in a specific direction to reach a destination. For example, a person driving in Cairo must have access to the recent street maps of Cairo to properly use the system. The alienated user is often unaware of the specific ways in which the GPS system works and the system's reliance on interconnected technologies and the user simply does not realize that the system is broken until the GPS tool directs the user to do such unexpected things like accidentally driving into a lake! Indeed, it was reported in 2008 that a Polish driver 'blindly' followed the instructions of a GPS system and drove his car into a lake because the GPS system was not updated with the correct and recent map information. It is easy and tempting to place fault on the machine in a case like this, but it is also important to recognize that a person who would be aware of the fact that a tool is malfunctioning is less likely to rely on the tool. Unfortunately, those who are operating at the third level of alienation, that is, not knowing whether a tool is functioning correctly, are unable to correctly make the judgement about the outcome of using a tool.

This level of alienation becomes especially critical when a tool is supposed to offer lifesaving results as in the case of some medical technologies. The users of most medical tools are specialists like doctors and nurses who would be expected to have overcome the level of alienation related to the function, use, and reliability of medical equipment. The matter becomes quite different when some of the technology passes into the hands of the alienated user who is unaware of the way in which the technology works or when the technology has gone bad. This is especially true in parts of the world where economic and political pressures could create conditions where the alienated user would be offered medical technology that is known to be malfunctioning. A common example of this process is the sale of expired medicines. Any medicine, from the pills one would take for a headache to the daily dose of medicine used to control hypertensions, represent a medical technology. The user must know how to take the medicine and when to take it, and an un-alienated user might even know how the medicine functions. However, most medicines have a lifetime indicated by the expiration date of the medicine, after which they cease to function in the way they were meant to. Indeed, some medicines might become harmful and poisonous after the expiration date, and the user of the medicine must know when the medicine has ceased to be useful. In many instances, the user is completely alienated from this component of the medicine, and there are reports of people taking expired medicines which have often led to death as in the case of a woman in Afghanistan who was unknowingly given expired malaria medication. Such tragic events point towards the dangers of operating in a system where the user of the technology remains alienated from the fact that the technology has ceased to work in the manner in which it was supposed to.

The connection between the second level of alienation, which related to understanding how a tool works, and the third level of orientation where the user must find ways of repairing the tool is the fact that the user must recognize that the tool is not doing what it was supposed to do. That aspect deals with the first level of alienation where the user must be able to clearly answer the question about the functions of the tool. For instance, a user must know that a GPS system is supposed to give correct directions to go from one place to another, and the user must have some sense of how the GPS system works, and then realize that the GPS system might not be giving the correct directions. At that point the user needs to find ways of repairing the tool. While it might appear that finding someone to repair a tool should be a relatively simple task, the increasing complexity of the tools around us makes it harder to clearly answer that question and overcome the third level of alienation and know for sure where to go to get a tool repaired. For most people this is a challenge that is met by simply turning to people around them who appear to know more about technology.

For instance, as a student, and later as a colleague, to other professors in a university I have had the interesting experience of being the de facto consultant for all matters technological. With training in one of the Indian Institutes of Technology, and as a teacher in a humanities department, surrounded by non-technologists, I have often been called upon to answer questions about tools that had stopped working. My colleagues were able to overcome the third level of alienation and were quick to identify when a tool was not functioning properly, and in many cases they would turn to me because they felt that I would be able to at least get it working for them to be able to continue with their work. Those who came to me for help had partly overcome the third level of alienation only because a person like me was in the vicinity. They did not, however, consider how well I was qualified to address their technological problems. Most people assume that if another person appears computer savvy, then that person must be able to solve *all* computer problems! Consequently, there are people in all organizations who would quickly become a local resource for fixing broken tools.

GETTING IT REPAIRED

This process becomes a veritable cottage industry where the persons who are doing the fixing might have little training about the tool, but have come to become recognized by their cohort as the expert. This phenomenon is the product of the alienated users partly overcoming the third level of alienation and turning to people they know to answer the question, "Who can fix this?" Finding the local help, even though the help might not be the best, is a step towards reducing the level of alienation. There is an increasing number of such users of technology who are able to overcome the first two levels of alienation and see that their tool has a significant amount of potential, but either all the functions are not working properly, or they want to ensure that all the functions are indeed being used to their best potential, and these users might not always know who to turn to for help, other than friends and colleagues. This tendency has been capitalized as witnessed in the growth of the number of Internet-based forums that offer help on technical issues where the ones seeking help can find others who might have special knowledge about the specific tools.

These Internet-based support systems are often called "forums" where online "friends" help each other to overcome the third level of alienation by constantly sharing information about the different ways to make specific tools work properly. These forums are, however, only useful if the user knows that something is wrong with the tool and is able and willing to turn to such forums for help. In many cases, there is an interaction between the members of the forum before a specific correct answer emerges. This is evident in the interchange below that was seen on one of the numerous forums about the iPhone:

08-21-2008, 01:58 PM #1
jman3715
Join Date: Aug 2008
Posts: 1 Deleting History

Let's just say (hypothetically) that you visited a site you may not be so proud of.
I deleted history but when I go back to the browser and type the first few letters in the address bar the old site shows up as an auto-complete option on the list.
I have cleared history, create a new page and X'd out the old one, rebooted the phone, but it just won't go away. I'm not talking about the google/yahoo bar but the address bar.
Any ideas how to clear out the auto complete history?
10-01-2008, 06:47 AM #2
cowalsh
Junior Member
Join Date: Sep 2008

Posts: 1 go to settings and clear out cookies and cache
0-25-2008, 03:12 AM #3
k3z6376
Junior Member
Join Date: Oct 2008
Posts: 11 You can clear cookies and cache but it will always go back to the last page u viewed.
0-27-2008, 02:08 AM #4
rafayj
Junior Member
Join Date: Oct 2008
Posts: 31 Click on File then settings then clear history and you would have ur history deleted.

Unlock iPhone 3G

What is especially important to note here is the fact that the interchange happens between "junior members" of the forum who are trying to help each other solve a specific problem with their gadget. All of the users have been able to overcome the third level of alienation and are able to at least ask the question about where to go to find a fix for the tool they are using. They are also familiar enough with the Internet to be able to seek the information from online resources. It is not always the case that users are able to use the Internet or any other resources to find someone who can fix a machine when the user is sure that the machine is not working properly. The third level of alienation is thus a function of the ways in which technology has developed leading to situations where the complexity of the tool makes it nearly impossible to correctly and effectively find the appropriate person to fix a machine. There are several reasons for this and the most important is the fact that the machines have become much too complex, as discussed earlier, to allow for a simple fix by a single person.

COMPLEX TOOLS NEEDING MULTIPLE HELPERS

It used to be the case that every big marketplace in cities and towns worldwide would have a clock-repair shop. These dusty old shops would have a wise old man (usually) who would be surrounded by hundreds of clocks. Such images would be remembered by people who used wrist watches, or clocks that had to be operated by winding up the clocks periodically. If one were to open up the inside of those clocks, there would be an intricate combination of springs and gears that kept the clock working properly and producing the once familiar 'tick tock' sound of the clock. Most importantly, the wrist watch or the pocket watch, immortalized by characters such as Sherlock Holmes and Hercules Poirot, were meant to do only one thing—tell time accurately. The clock repairer would work with a technology that was ages old and had remained largely unchanged. Although there are conflicting accounts of the origins of the spring-driven clock, it is clear that clocks were popular in the thirteenth century when the precursor of the modern clock was adopted. Many different kinds of clocks were produced from that early inception, and places like Salar Jung Museum in Hyderabad, India and the clock towers in Munich, Germany and Prague, Czech Republic have preserved clocks from many different generations to show people that the original clock was a complex machine but was used to do only the task of keeping time accurately. If the clock failed to do that, it would be considered unusable. There was little scope of ambiguity about the first and second levels of alienation with the tool. Most users knew what the tool was supposed to do and most knew that the clock was built around a series of complex springs just as most people realized when the clock was not working and had a good sense that the neighborhood clock repair shop would be able to repair the clock.

Starting in late 1960s a new way of keeping time was popularized by the Seiko Company of Japan with the introduction of the Astron wristwatch that used a quartz crystal to keep time, instead of a spring that needed to be wound up periodically. This marked the beginning of the shift from a mechanical watch to an electronic watch, where the springs would become increasingly redundant. The springs would eventually disappear from watches altogether and the face of the watch would change, from the circle with 12 digits and three hands, to a display of numbers that would exactly show the time. The old clock repairer who honed his art on tiny springs and levers was suddenly not the right person to turn to when the clock stopped working. This shift to electronic clocks also marked a significant point in the timekeeping technology because the watch could now be built around a microprocessor[19] that was capable of doing much more than reporting the correct time. The excess capacity of the tiny computer in a simple watch was quickly harnessed to do other tasks such as report the day, date, and year in the case of the wristwatch along with the capability of acting as a stopwatch to precisely measure the time it takes for an event to happen. The traditional personal watch with one little winding knob on the right side was replaced by numerous little push buttons which could be used to provide different kinds of information that could be displayed on a digital readout that replaced the watch hands. Through this sophistication the watch converged into a much more complicated tool that was capable of doing many more things than what the traditional watch was expected to do. The process of convergence could bring certain advantages as discussed in Chapter 2, but it also automatically made the tool more complicated.

Such examples of tools becoming complicated are even more pronounced in the case of larger machines such as cars and complicated tools like computers. The traditional car, as discussed earlier, was easy to fathom and thus easy to fix because one single person was often knowledgeable enough to be able to fix the problems with the simpler machines. Other tools such as the PC is a complex assembly of different parts that must work together effectively to make it useful and each of the parts could require different kinds of training to identify and correct problems. In the case of computers, this division is most pronounced in the way in which people are trained to become computer specialists. Engineering and science institutions, ranging from the Indian Institutes of Technology to the Massachusetts Institute of Technology, have different kinds of specializations that produce differently trained people who might all eventually be responsible for the design of a single complex tool. In the case of computer training, this distinction is seen between the computer programmer who works best with the software or computer programs and the computer engineer who deals primarily with the hardware or the actual objects that can be found in the computer. This distinction demonstrates that the person who is trying to overcome the third level of alienation soon realizes that there is no single person who can magically repair a non-working tool. In most cases, the user needs to have overcome the first two levels of alienation to know who the right person is for repairing the tool.

When dealing with such complex tools, it becomes essential to completely answer the question related to the purpose of the tool and to generally answer the question related to how the tool works to know all the functions of the complex tool and then identify what exactly is not working. This is best illustrated with computers. Many who have used a PC using the Windows software are familiar with a phenomenon called the "Blue Screen of Death (BSOD)" that happens when the computer malfunctions and ceases to work. At that instant, the computer screen displays a bright blue color with cryptic messages on the screen before shutting down. These messages could be statements like, "IRQL_NOT_LESS_OR_EQUAL" or "KMODE_EXCEPTION_NOT_HANDLED" that would be complete gibberish to most users. Yet this is a problem that shows up on any computer that uses the Windows system. In an infamous event the computer that runs some of the light displays at New York's Times Square suffered from problems and the unintelligible entries related to BSOD were displayed in a huge display in Times Square. The interesting thing about the BSOD is the messages that are displayed on the screen and the information it conveys to the users. For users who have overcome the first two levels of alienation, it becomes clear that fixing the problem could involve repairing different aspects of the problem and one single person might not be able to do the complete repair.

Situations like the BSOD demonstrate that at the third level of alienation the user must be able to correctly answer who the correct person is for repairing the complex tools that surround us. The appropriateness of the person is not only based on the exact nature of the problem but also related to the way level of expertise the person has in using tools that would be used to fix the problem. Machines now are so dependant on other tools that the correct person without the correct tools might still not be able to fix the problem. Therefore, the complexity of the gadgets that surround us pose a dual problem when they need repair—first there must be a group of people who know how to fix the machine and that group must possess the right tools to be able to deal with the problem. The user, on the other hand, needs to overcome the level of alienation and figure out who the appropriate team is to fix the problem after the user realizes that the gadget needs to be fixed.

TEAMS WITH TOOLS

The complexity of the machines that create the third level of alienation has led to the development of specific organizations that have become the central points for fixing broken machines. One of the best illustrations of this comes from the automobile industry. A modern car is made up of thousands of interrelated parts. All of the units of the car must work together in perfect unison for the machine to work in the way intended. These parts are increasingly hidden from the user who is usually only expected to use the car and not try to tinker with it, let alone fix it. The user must, however, be able to tell when the car is not operating as it should. In some of the older cars, such as the Ambassador of India or the Austin of England, it was possible for the user to look under the hood and see the parts, and often become familiar with the parts and identify some of the problems to eventually fix the problem. For example, older cars would have belts that would connect different parts of the engine, and a typical driver would be able to look under the hood and realize that a particular belt was torn and perhaps replace that belt. Even if the user did not want to do the work, there were always people, often called "mechanics," who were adept at fixing all the problems with cars. These people would have little shops where they would have numerous decrepit looking cars that were all being fixed by the same person, or the same small group of people. Growing up in Calcutta, India, I remember our family had an old Standard Herald car modeled after the Triumph series of British cars, and whenever it would malfunction (which it seemed to quite a bit) my father would take it to the same mechanic operating on Jessore Road and that mechanic would fix the car. The mechanic became similar to the family doctor who would know all the idiosyncrasies of the specific car. My father, like many others who had cars, was sufficiently un-alienated at the third level to actually tell the mechanic what was most likely wrong with the car. Indeed, repairing the car was a consultative process with much looking under and around the car as my father and the mechanic would come to a decision about the course of action to heal the car.

Such collaborative repair has become impossible with the complexity of the car where the user is always partly alienated at the second level because it is often difficult to tell what indeed is wrong with the car. The usual indicators of odd sounds, strange movements and unusual handling do not offer sufficient information for the user to know what the precise problem is. It is nearly impossible to look for these problems by a visual examination of the vehicle, except for something obvious such as a flat tire! Yet, if the problem remains unchecked it could result in a situation where the vehicle will simply stop working. The automobile industry is increasingly aware of this issue of alienation and it has started to make some moves that help the alienated user. One of the most popular strategies has been indicator lamps that warn the user of impending problems. These indicators would say things like "check engine" and a bright orange light would appear in the instrument panel of the car. Such cryptic and ambiguous messages, almost similar to the BSOD messages, certainly do not help to reduce the alienation of the user, especially when the user can feel nothing wrong with the car. In a 2003 article in the *New York Times*, Jim Motavalli joked about this warning sign in saying:

> The light may mean many things. One frequent problem, for example, is that the emissions system is off kilter, and the car is polluting the air; another is that the gasoline cap is loose, causing the car's computer to detect an unusual pressure level in the tank (tighten it and the light will eventually go off). But the glitches that activate the check-engine light are often nothing a driver would readily notice. As a result, the country is full of people driving around with check-engine lights aglow—often while trying to figure out how to shut them off.

The important issues here are that the driver cannot easily fix the problems and the driver does not even know the exact nature of the problem to decide who to take the car to. A person who can fix the emission system is not the one who can fix the engine. This is the classic case of the third level of alienation.

The check-engine light and the BSOD in the case of the computer all eventually point towards the user having to take the malfunctioning machine to a place where a group of trained people have the appropriate tools to diagnose the problem and then fix it. The mechanic that used to work on our family car used his sensory tools—listen for the odd click or watch for the patch of oil under the car—to make most of the diagnoses. The modern car, from which the driver is increasingly alienated, has special receptacles that allow the trained repair people to plug in cables and computers that would help diagnose the problem that might have triggered the check-engine warning or the BSOD in the computer. Fixing such problems requires other machines which will first allow the fixer to identify the problem. The machines that do this are expensive and complicated and operators of these diagnostic tools need training to be able to even identify the nature of the problem.

After the problem has been located further tools are needed to fix the problem. A simple wrench, hammer and screwdriver are not sufficient to repair the machine. The complexity of the machine makes it imperative that specific and appropriate gadgets are used to repair the problem. This has led to the development of the registered repair centers such as car dealerships where the dealer has the tools and the trained personnel to fix the cars or computers. In the case of cars, the dealership is increasingly replacing the traditional mechanic who was adept enough to work on many different cars. For example, in India during the 1960s and 1970s, there were about four to five different kinds of cars that were popular and the roadside mechanic could repair any type of car.[20] That mechanic has now been replaced by dealerships as many more kinds of cars have entered the marketplace and each needs its own kind of diagnostic tools and specially trained persons. The method of repair that required interplay between the user and the mechanic has disappeared because that user is increasingly alienated and the mechanic neither has the tools nor the specialized knowledge required to work on a broken machine. The dealership has taken on a central role as users have been increasingly experiencing the third level of alienation from the machines that people rely on for their everyday work.

The idea of the dealership, or teams with tools, is connected to what Arnold Pacey, author of *The Culture of Technology*, has called the "culture of expertise" in his book. As users are increasingly alienated, Pacey has argued that there has developed a cultural system where the user has to depend on experts who know how specific tools work and how the machines can be repaired. There is thus a plethora of dealers which has mushroomed all over the world that advertises themselves as approved service centers for brand name items. There has emerged a close connection between brand names and expertise where the owner of a Honda vehicle will have to take the car to a Honda dealer for repairs since no other car mechanic would have the appropriate tools and knowledge to repair the car. Part of the knowledge relates to understanding what is wrong with a car. For instance, if one has a Toyota car, then the manufacturer uses proprietary computer software that controls many of the activities of the car. Only Toyota dealers have the computer diagnostic tools that let them diagnose the reason for the check-engine light coming on. Even if the reason is as mundane as the cap to the petrol tank being loose, the user would have to pay a hefty sum at the dealership to get the diagnosis done and then tighten the cap! This is a direct consequence of the second and third levels of alienation since the user is basically unable to figure out exactly what is wrong with the machine and thus has limited options about selecting the repair person. The effect of dealerships has been felt most in the developed countries as evidenced in efforts towards legislation demonstrated in the following quote from a 2008 news story in the *New York Times* about a new law in the state of New Jersey in the United States:

> The State Assembly yesterday passed legislation that, if signed into law, would give motorists the ability to obtain all information necessary for the diagnosis, service and repair of their vehicles—thus eliminating the need for a trip to a specific dealership for routine maintenance and repairs.

Such moves would allow the users to be little less alienated from their tools since the user would gain greater information. This tendency towards developing a culture of dealerships has percolated to many other industries like the computer dealerships and service centers that focus on specific makes of computers, dealers for cell phones which can repair specific phones, dealers for home appliances and dealers for numerous other gadgets that surround us.

The teams with tools not only provide the tools for the repair but also the culture of expertise migrates to the knowledge and training that the workers in the team have. The traditional car mechanic was trained "on the job." Cars did not change dramatically between different models. In India, for instance, the Ambassador car stayed virtually the same for nearly two decades. That tendency has started to change as more machines are built with obsolescence in mind. As discussed in Chapter 2, more tools are now being built where the machine is expected to become obsolete within a short period of time. Innovations in technology allow manufacturers to build in special features and the marketing associated with technology can convince buyers to upgrade frequently. While in most cases such upgrades are beneficial, it is the case that the user is increasingly alienated at the third level as the new tools are adopted. As a consequence of the constant upgrades and changes, only the repair personnel with the dealerships are able to maintain the level of expertise needed to do repairs. The independent mechanic, who could fix any car with any problem, quickly becomes a relic because they simply cannot maintain the level of skills needed to work with the complicated machines. In many ways, the changes to technology also alienate the people who might have been experts very recently.

The third level of alienation becomes especially difficult to overcome for the user because of the need for the specialized training that the average user would not have. Even if the user is able to get to a point where the first two levels of alienation have been overcome with a specific tool, the user might never be able to fully overcome the third level of alienation to make a truly informed decision about the best way of repairing a malfunctioning tool. The user increasingly looses control on the process of repair and has to rely on the limited number of choices that are provided by the manufacturer and dealer. This lack of choice could easily lead to a situation where the user does not even want to deal with the issue of getting a machine repaired, but would simply choose the simpler path of discarding the malfunctioning tool and replacing it with a new tool that serves the same functions as the old tool. This is easier to do with some kinds of machines than others. It is far more difficult to replace a nonworking car with a new one because the costs of a new car could be far higher than the price of a repair, but with many gadgets the alienated user might simply choose to remain alienated and replace a gadget as soon as it stops functioning in the expected way.

REPLACE, NOT REPAIR

The tendency to replace a tool instead of repairing it stems from two interrelated facts. The first issue has to do with the third level of alienation where the user is unable to satisfactorily answer the question, "Who can fix this tool?" The frustration related to realizing that the tool is not functioning properly and the fact that it is difficult to find a repair person often leads to the decision to replace. The second factor relates to the ease with which it is possible to replace as opposed to the difficulties with repair. It is often much simpler to walk into a store and buy a newer version of the tool than to try and repair the old one. The pricing structure of many of the gadgets that surround us has been designed to encourage replacement over repair. It is interesting to note that many American stores that sell electronics would have price lists for guaranteeing a product beyond the meager 90-day warranty that most manufacturers provide. The consumer can therefore purchase additional warranties for two, three, and five years that guarantee that they will not have to pay anything if the gadget malfunctions within that time period. In most cases, however, the guarantee is to replace the gadget and not to repair it. The total expense of repairing a malfunctioning tool is far greater for the company that makes the tool, and it is much more cost effective to offer the consumer a brand new product. The consumer/user is also often much happier with the new product as opposed to getting the older one fixed. The new product not only has the aura of newness but also most often functions in the same way as the old one, perhaps with some minor improvements. The user does not feel the sense of alienation because the difference between the products is marginal and so a satisfied user is able to obtain all the functionalities without having to worry about the third level of alienation.

The tendency to simply replace a tool without attempting to overcome the third level of alienation has interesting implications for the user, the technology industry, and the way in which the tool is marketed to the user. For the user, the tool becomes primarily a system that fulfils certain functionalities and the value of the tool is in the fact that it is able to do a certain set of things. The ability to decide between the replace and repair options assumes that the user actually has largely overcome the first two levels of alienation. They have a fairly good idea of what a tool is meant to do and are also able to recognize the condition when the tool fails to perform. However, the option to replace allows the user to be able to solve the problem of the non-working tool without ever having to consider what is wrong with the tool and how it might be fixed. There is a great danger in this because the replacement might be simply unnecessary because the malady with the tool is so minor that successfully overcoming the third level of alienation could sway the decision towards the repair option as opposed to the replace option.

However, more tools are manufactured in a way where either the manufacturer has actively discouraged repair, or made it impossible.

For example, in late 2007, a new form of digital camera appeared in the market. This was sold as a throwaway camera that had the single function of taking a set of digital pictures that could be printed out directly from the camera. Once the limited set of pictures were printed out, the camera had no further functionality. It was not that the camera was malfunctioning, but the camera had exhausted its functionality and the user would not even have to worry about the third level of alienation, but would simply throw the camera away. This is how the tool was actually promoted and advertised. In this case, the manufacturer has effectively solved the problem of the third level of alienation by never placing the users in a position where they would have to figure who can "fix" the tool. In some cases, the camera might quit working as expected even before the limited number of pictures were taken. While that could annoy the user for not being able to print the pictures, the camera was priced so affordably that throwing it away was not a huge strain on resources. This was an inexpensive tool that was meant to be replaced when its functionality was over. As long as the user could overcome the first and second levels of alienation they would be satisfied consumers.

The situation is quite different when the tool is more expensive and the economic aspect leads the user to consider overcoming the third level of alienation. Consider, for example, the computer I am using to compose this manuscript. It is a very complex and relatively expensive machine and if it were to stop working, I would probably choose to take it to a friend or colleague (or myself, who is quite adept with computers!) Such a person would be able to open the computer enclosure and would most likely be able to do sufficient repairs at a reasonable cost so that I would not have to replace the machine. There is, however, a problem with the way in which the machine is guaranteed by the manufacturer. It says on the back of the machine, right next to the screws that would have to be opened to reach inside the machine, "No user serviceable parts inside." And it warns that if the screws are opened by a non-licensed technician, then the guarantee would be voided. This is clear discouragement for the user to overcome the third level of alienation in any way other than resorting to the dealer as discussed earlier in the chapter. The dealer, as pointed out earlier, automatically makes the job much more expensive.

The issue of cost and benefit often becomes the key motivation for seeking to overcome the third level of alienation because the cost of the alienation could be unbearably high. This is demonstrated in a news article that appeared in an American newspaper called the *Pittsburgh Tribune News* in 2008. In the face of a global economic recession, many consumers were actually opting for the repair option since this was more cost effective. The news story quoted a car repair person who said, "We are seeing a lot of people more interested in repairing their car rather than taking the easy option of buying."[21] What is specially important to note is the fact that this statement comes from a non-dealer repair person who was getting more business in the lean times because people began to overcome the third level of alienation and began to answer the question about fixing a machine in a more informed and careful manner. It is quite likely, however, that in better economic times, the user would probably select to replace a malfunctioning machine even if it were an expensive machine.

One of the most important things to note about the third level of alienation is the fact that this alienation is fundamentally different from the first two levels where the locus of the alienation was in the relationship between the user and the machine. A user who was truly interested in overcoming the first two levels would have to be able to do so with some degree of reflection and research. In some cases, the industry that produced the particular tool also took an interest in helping people overcome the first two levels of alienation. That relationship shifts at the third level where the problem becomes multifaceted and the relationship between the machine and the user is supplemented by the relationship between the user and the industrial system that helps to make and promote a machine. A look at any daily newspaper anywhere in the world would demonstrate this process where numerous attractive advertisements of cell phones would remind the consumer that the old cell phone is essentially malfunctioning because it does not have all the functionalities of the new and improved one. In urging the consumer to upgrade, the industry encourages the third level of alienation, posing specific hurdles in the way of the user.

The process is further supported by ancillary industries that almost conspire to keep the user alienated. Consider, for instance, the large cottage industry in "exchange schemes" that is popular in countries like India. As a rapidly growing economy, with a middle-class the size of the entire American population, there is a huge amount of disposable income that the consumer is willing to spend on technology. I was at a furniture exhibition in Calcutta, India in the winter of 2008 where under one roof it was possible to inspect the best of the new appliances that could adorn the Indian kitchen which has been plagued by machines that seemed to constantly require repair forcing the consumer to overcome the third level of alienation. This situation is being remedied by manufacturers and distributors who are willing to offer attractive pricing schemes where they would offer a discount for the new appliance, if the consumer is willing to trade in the old appliance. The older machine would then be refurbished and resold to a different market segment. Such offers appear extremely attractive to some consumers because the consumers not only feel that they have received a good deal but also do not have to go through the frustration related to overcoming the third level of alienation.

Similar programs have appeared across the globe as the industry helps to alleviate consumer anxiety. A website called

"Buymytronics" offers consumers attractive prices for malfunctioning equipment. A report about the site gives examples of the amount of money that people have made, "A broken iPod went for $228. They gave a customer $210 for a used BlackBerry. And one consumer walked away with $250 for an unwanted Xbox 360." Such programs are not directly run by the technology industry, but allow the industry to encourage a level of alienation where the consumer has limited options when answering the question about the best way of repairing a tool.

A user who is able to overcome the first two levels of alienation could still be stuck at the third level of alienation and would never overcome that level of alienation and would constantly have to choose between the dealer and replacement. However, some users are able to see the possible answers to the key question at the third level of alienation and could well overcome this level of alienation by simply realizing that there are a limited number of responses to the question. At that moment, they could enter the final level of alienation and ask the crucial question, "Can I fix this broken tool?" This is explored in the next chapter.

5

I Can Fix This

As a youngster I had got into trouble many times for breaking household gadgets like tape recorders, toasters, record players and anything that had a screw that could be opened with a screwdriver. The general trend was that a piece of equipment would stop working and most of the members in the home would be somewhat puzzled—remaining at the second or third level of alienation—and would not be totally sure about whether to replace the malfunctioning gadget or to try and repair it. Although in India the answer was often to repair it, there was the level of alienation where it was unclear as to who the appropriate person would be to do the repair. In the 1970s, the machines were starting to get more complicated than what the corner shop electrician could repair, and so there was often the case when the gadget was replaced, and the old one was packed up and put away in some dark corner of the kitchen or in some storage box. I would then have the opportunity to pick the gadget up and ask the question that deals with overcoming the final level of alienation, "Can I fix this?"

Those who have overcome the initial levels of alienation and are able to recognize that the machine is malfunctioning reach the point where they are willing to deal with the issue of finding the correct person to repair the machine before deciding to replace. At that point, there are some who are un-alienated enough to think of fixing the machine themselves. Based on the preliminary assumptions of the laws of alienation, those who are able to affirmatively say that they can fix the machine themselves have reached a sense of closeness to the tool that allows them specific powers where the gadget has lost its aura and mystery and the user has gained mastery over the tool instead of remaining alienated from the tool. The ability to answer the question is, however, dependant on a series of factors, some of which are based on the person and others in the way in which technology and tools have evolved. These factors are the focus of this chapter.

Returning, however, to the personal tale of wanting to fix the broken machines, I should note that this tendency was by no means unique to me. It is often the case that there are children who are prone to explore mechanical things (and now, electronic gadgets) because they are driven by the natural curiosity that is the hallmark of any child. There are different manifestations of curiosity in children, but without curiosity one would not learn, and in trying to fix machines, I and many others were actually simply giving in to the curiosity. I was never sure whether I would be able to fix the machine, although on occasion I would be able to do that, to the awe of the grown ups, but what I was in the process of doing was reduce my alienation from the machine. Since the machine was already relegated to the junk heap, there was no fear that I could do anything worse to the machine and was thus allowed by my parents to mess with it. It was a completely different case with machines that were working properly. My screwdriver and I were explicitly instructed not to touch things, perhaps because I was prone to open things up, as long as they were working properly. Part of the reason for this level of alienation is precisely based on the tendency to disallow experimentation with gadgets because people are taught to be scared of the machines, and are encouraged not to ask the question, "Can I fix this?" There is a specific fear that is systematically built into people, especially within children, which is supposed to encourage conformity with the alienated and discourage curiosity.

FEAR OF TECHNOLOGY

The process of alienation that has been described across all the former chapters can be traced to a fundamental human emotion—fear. Human beings are hardwired to be afraid, because fear offers a basic survival instinct called "flight." When any animal is scared, especially for its life, a very animal instinct is triggered that leads the animal to flee from the cause of fear. It is only when that flight is not possible that the animal might act in self-defense and might confront the source of the fear. There is a further refinement of the fight or flight response in humans where physicians and psychologists agree that the body responds to environmental threat by selecting the flight or fight response when the body is faced with a stressful situation. Specific hormones such as adrenalin are secreted in the body preparing it to either fight the threat or quickly flee from it. In either case, the body must recognize the threat to be something dangerous and then decide to flee. Recognition of danger and threat thus becomes critical to the process of deciding to stay or leave the fray. Many would simply flee from what is perceived as dangerous or fearful without attempting to understand the cause and source of the fear.

The issue of fear is closely associated with the notion of alienation from technology at all levels of alienation, and it can be argued that people are often fearful of technology and could get so apprehensive about the use of a tool that they would simply choose not to use it. The matter of fear becomes far more critical at the final level of alienation where the user of the technology is sufficiently fearful of the technology that they choose not to attempt to fix the broken tool because of the fear of making the matter worse or running into insurmountable challenges as the user tries to repair the tool. This fear of attempting to fix a broken tool is often based on a societal system where the fear might have been created through a system of processes where fear of technology—at least the process of fixing it—becomes ingrained through a series of practices that creates the alienation at this level.

As discussed earlier in the book, one of the principal ways in which the fear of personal fixes to a tool is generated involves the manufacturers of the tool who often explicitly state that there is no way for the user to fix the tool. In making statements that warn the user of voiding a warranty, the maker of the tool is deliberately discouraging the user from doing anything with the broken tool other than taking it to an expert ratified by the manufacturer. The culture of expertise built around the dealership becomes the only answer to the broken tool specially if the tool is expensive and the user feels that there is a risk in attempting to repair the tool because it could easily lead to greater complications with the tool and the manufacturer. A combination of fear and high risk perception often convinces a user that it is best not to attempt to fix the tool. The fear associated with repair is also played up in other warning signs where statements on the gadget might actually warn the user of bodily harm if the user were to attempt to repair the tool. In some electrical appliances it is not unusual to see signs that warn the user of the possible risks of electrocution if the user were to tinker with the machinery. The language of the warning is often explicit and certainly scary as in the case of electric heaters which could state that the user would get a nasty electrical shock or burn a limb by incorrect handling of the gadget. Such statements are used to generate the level of alienation that will discourage a user of the tool from attempting to fix it themselves.

In some cases the warning statements are quite valid and make logical sense because some of the users might be alienated at different levels and could do things that would certainly put a person in a dangerous position. For example, a person who does not fully understand how a specific tool works and is thus alienated from the tool could attempt to repair an electrical tool without unplugging it from the electrical outlet and could electrocute themselves. A simple example of this process is seen when a person would use a metal object like a fork or spoon to extricate a toast stuck inside a toaster. Even though the toaster might not be red hot, it could be plugged into the electrical outlet and a person could accidentally get a fatal electrical shock when trying to "repair" the toaster and pull out a toast. Similar other attempts to repair electrical tools can lead to dangerous outcomes and manufacturers are compelled to discourage the user from attempting such personal repairs.

Scaring the user into alienation is also the product of the ways in which alienated users might have responded to the results of botched attempts to repair a tool. In societies that are increasingly litigious, users might actually do something that is relatively unwise and then bring a law suit against the manufacturer for not adequately warning the user about the dangers of the trying to repair the tool. Although there are no specific cases that deal with users suing a corporation for failing to warn against the dangers of self-repair, there are sufficient examples of corporations being brought to court for failing to warn about the negative effects of the use of technology. This has been especially true for companies that manufacture medicines and might have failed to provide warnings about the side effects of the use of the medicine leading to users eventually bringing class action law suits where the corporations have been significantly fined for failing to warn. Many such examples have led manufacturers to err on the safe side and offer as many warnings as possible that can generate a sufficient fear of the machinery and people would think before attempting to overcome the level of alienation where the user would attempt to repair a broken gadget.

The fear of technology is also produced by other societal tendencies where people are conditioned into alienation, where the user would not take the risk of attempting to fix the broken machine. These fears are not necessarily produced by warning signs on equipment but by a conditioning where people are taught to be fearful of tools and are taught to be respectful of the magical machines that have become a part of everyday life. Children are told to stay away from the machines and are often berated if they are found to be messing with a precious piece of machinery. Many of these fears stem from the basic levels of alienation where many people are so alienated from the tools that they are simply scared to see someone naively dealing with a tool which seems hugely complicated. Many will remember childhood days when the natural curiosity of being a child would lead a youngster to tinker with the tools that surrounded us, but were often told by the older people not to touch the expensive tools. The primary antidote to alienation—the natural human curiosity—was effectively squashed producing greater degrees of fear where people would be trained to be fearful of the tools. This fear has very little to do with the way in which the machine is made or works, but is produced by a process where the alienation experienced by some is propagated to others in the process of formal and informal instruction.

The process of teaching to be fearful of technology is similar to the way in which specific societal roles are acquired by children. In many societies it is often the case that the female child is especially encouraged to be fearful of tools whereas the male child could be allowed to experiment more with gadgets and tools. It is not surprising that there has been a woeful lack of female applicants and students in institutions of engineering like the Indian Institutes of Technology not because women were academically unprepared to be an engineer but the same fear that creates the technological alienation also propagated the myth that women should be fearful of tools. Many aspects of society, from the kinds of toys that children are given to the kinds of professions that people are encouraged to follow, are motivated by the general sense that there are accepted ways of doing things and being fearful of dealing with tools is conventional.

With the increasing popularity of different kinds of gadgets it is, however, becoming more difficult to create a level of alienation where people are discouraged from using tools. The industrial forces manufacturing iPhones and similar gadgets want the largest possible penetration of their products. The manufacturers do not want to be hamstrung by barriers of gender, race, and other demographic determinants. The fear of technology primarily extends to the issue of overcoming the level of alienation where the user is discouraged from affirmatively answering the question, "Can I fix this?" The general accepted notion is that being able to use a tool does not provide the expertise to be able to fix it. To be sure, this is true for many kinds of tools. For instance, the driver of an automobile might simply not be trained to repair the automobile, and many people clearly recognize the limits of their abilities to do certain things. In some cases there could be real risks related to attempting to repair specific tools because there are significant dangers to the process. There are reports of cases where people trying to repair tools such as electric saws and knives have gravely injured themselves by accidentally doing something that has led to injury. There are instances of people accidentally shooting another person with a gun when trying to fix a gun that was not functioning properly. Fears related to such situations are certainly valid, and the reason of the fear is embedded in specific experiences. That is significantly different from the process where the alienation is the product of specific accepted practices that teach people to remain alienated from tools when it comes to dealing with the repair of the tool. It is especially difficult to overcome this level of alienation because there are significant indicators that suggest that one can do grave harm in trying to fix technological problems and such activities should actually only be done by experts. Often a few bad experiences with trying to repair things only feed into the fear that is produced conventionally.

<hr>

BAD EXPERIENCE

A bad experience with attempting to repair machinery by overcoming the level of alienation discussed here can take different forms. One common bad experience is one where not only does the repair process not fix the machine but also makes it even worse leading to a great deal of frustration on the part of the user. This is why many user guides for repairing computer problems often warn the user that they must save their critical data in a secure way before attempting to correct problems with the computer. Consider for instance the situation of a user who might be attempting to repair a computer that has been afflicted with a computer virus. Most Windows-based computers have an internal program called the registry and all the functions of the computer are controlled by the instructions included in the registry file. A corruption of the registry file could lead to a computer going completely out of order. Yet, some virus removal processes require making some major changes to the registry and in most cases the repair process begins with the instruction of saving the existing registry file to protect the user against corrupting the registry file so badly that things actually get worse. Similar situations occur with tools that have mechanical components where the user might damage one part of the tool while trying to repair another. These mistakes result in bad experiences where the user feels that they probably ought not to have tried to repair the problem at all and ought to have either replaced the machine or taken it to a dealer. These problems could be the result of simple mistakes and do not necessarily reflect a lack of aptitude on the part of the user but could be caused by a myriad of reasons, but all result in perpetuating the fear that is the barrier against overcoming the alienation that is associated with attempting to repair a tool. The user often is disheartened by the inability to repair the tool and carries that memory which discourages future attempts. For example, a child who has a toy that has stopped working could, out of curiosity, try to repair the toy, but realize on opening up the toy that it is very difficult to repair and thus decide not to try such repairs in the future. The key issue with personal repairs going bad is the fact that the individual often personalizes the experience and exaggerates the alienation from technology. In most cases the blame for failing to repair the tool is characterized as a personal failing with the user feeling that it is the person's incompetence that made matters worse. This technological persecution is evident in statements such as, "I did not know what I was doing," or "I was not smart enough to repair the tool." This is the point at which the fear of technology is reinforced. In some cases this self-blaming can actually be so strong that it results in an increased fear of technology, specially if the failed attempts to repair the problem result in increased cost of eventual repair by a specialist, or if a piece of equipment is destroyed to a point where it is beyond repair. Recently, my teenage son acquired a small air pistol that would shoot plastic pellets. All of a sudden it got jammed, and he decided to try and open up the shooter and attempt to extricate the jammed element. The result, unfortunately, was that he completely disassembled the toy and was unable to put it together, making a pile of junk that had to be thrown away, completely writing off a marginally expensive purchase. The experience, however, resulted in a decision of not trying to do this again, since my son took on the blame for causing the expensive mistake. What was interesting to note, however, is that he tried to do the entire repair with a pair of scissors and a knife that served as a screwdriver. What remains unclear in such situations is whether the repairer was inept, or if the repairer was equipped with incorrect tools.

One of the ironies of the level of alienation where a person is attempting to repair a tool is that the user must have overcome alienation with other tools that are required to do the repair. The tool for the repair takes on a significant importance when considering the level of alienation where the user is scared to do a repair. As discussed earlier, most gadgets need some tools that are required to understand the problem with the gadget and eventually repair it. Consider the common occurrence of getting a flat tire when driving a car. In some countries the roads are so treacherous that it is a relatively common phenomenon and the owner or the driver of the vehicle could easily find oneself in the position of having to do a repair where the flat tire would have to be removed from the car and be replaced with a spare tire that might be in the car. This process is impossible to do without the availability of a tool that is often called a "jack" that can be correctly placed under the vehicle to raise the car to a comfortable level where the offending tire can be removed from the car and the good tire be put back. Additionally, this task requires a tool that would allow the user to be able to unscrew the bolts that hold the tire to the car and usually the human hand is not sufficiently strong to do this task without the correct tool. This illustrates a situation where a user who has overcome the alienation related to personally repairing a tool is still stumped because the user might not have the right tools in the car. Sometimes, having the tool is also not sufficient if the repair tool is itself faulty or inappropriate. The situation with my son trying to repair a toy with a knife and a scissor, when indeed a screwdriver and pliers was called for, demonstrates how a user might remain alienated because they simply had the completely wrong equipment to work with. Most of the time, the choice of wrong equipment is the result of lack of access to the right equipment. The creative person who is trying to overcome this level of alienation could try to substitute the appropriate tools with whatever is conveniently available, but in doing so, the person could increase the sense of alienation because the repair attempt could be completely undermined because of the lack of appropriate tools, and the user still ends up blaming oneself for the failure even though the real reason was the lack of appropriate tools.

The issue of appropriate tools needs to be considered carefully since there are many instances where the appropriate tool is also very specialized. The jack used to raise a car for changing out a flat tire is a good example of the specialization. The jack is supposed to hold the car up, defying gravity, while the tire is being changed. A jack that easily holds up a behemoth like a Toyota Innova or a Honda Odyssey, both being rather large vans, would not suffice for a Tata Motors Nano car or the Smart car being popularized in Europe and America. Without the correct and specialized tools, it would be impossible to effectively overcome the level of alienation that moves a person from being the victim of new tools to one who is able to tackle problems with the new tools without having to constantly turn to the so-called experts who have the advantage of having the correct tools to do the repair.

Lack of appropriate tools ends up being a significant barrier to overcoming the level of alienation where a person is unable to affirmatively answer the question related to the person's ability to repair a tool. This signifies a very important aspect of alienation because the user is fundamentally giving up control on technological destiny and accepting the fact that the user is unable to help in the situation where a technological artefact ceases to function. This could well create a sense of failure where the people who failed begin to believe that they are technologically alienated with respect to fixing a failing tool and are thus in some way inferior to those who would take on the challenge of repairing the tool, even if the process destroyed the item. At this level of alienation, based on negative experiences with attempting to work with technological systems, a clearly defined class system is being put in place, particularly for youngsters, where the "smart" kids could do the miraculous repairs and get the music system working again, whereas, the other kids would open up the gadget and destroy it beyond reasonable repair. This dichotomy becomes a pivotal point in childhood, and those kids who can make the toaster pop often are acknowledged for their aptitude, thus propagating the idea that those who cannot innovate are necessarily inferior. In reality, however, the failings often lie in places distinct from the person because technological systems have become so complex that many components of the system remain inaccessible to the user.

KEEPING THINGS HIDDEN

One such area of problem is the lack of documentation that is provided with the complex gadgets that surround us. There was a time when new gadgets were always accompanied with detailed user's manuals that would lay out the operating instructions and would also include information on a variety of "troubleshooting" options that would allow the user to do small repairs without having to turn to experts and dealers. In some cases the documentation would also provide information about the kinds of tools required to do repair and maintenance on the tool, making the entire technological system accessible to the user. That tendency has been replaced by eliminating the detailed information when a gadget is sold. Most technical items are sold with simplified instructions that assume that the user is always alienated from the technology and need not have any more information than what is barely essential to operate the tool. The computer industry has specially streamlined the process of eliminating detailed instructions. Most computers are now sold with a foldout poster-like piece of paper that has step-by-step instructions, along with pictures, that tell the user how to set up the machine for basic use. There is no further information about how the machine works or what the specific components of the machine do. If the user wants further information then one would have to dig through multiple pages of websites where a more detailed user manual could be included. This tendency necessarily alienates the user when it comes to doing simple repairs. The complete lack of documentation forces the courageous user to attempt to fix complex machines without having a clear notion of what is inside the machine, and what the different parts of the machine do. When such "working in the dark" repair fails, it is often due to the lack of information rather than a lack of expertise on the part of the user. It is quite possible that those users who would have detailed information as was provided in earlier user manuals would have a better chance at overcoming the level of alienation where the user becomes fearful about repairing a tool.

The issue with manuals is also symptomatic of another problem that leads to alienation since the machines have become increasingly complex and are manufactured in ways where the different components become so well integrated with each other that it becomes a daunting task for an everyday user to repair the machine. The machines are designed to be inaccessible. One of the areas where this becomes especially evident is with automobiles. As discussed earlier in the book, car manufacturers have increasingly moved on to an integrated engine where all the major components of the engine are molded into one large piece of metal and it is nearly impossible to reach any specific component of the engine as was the case with earlier cars. Growing up in India, many like me who entered the age of technological curiosity in the 1960s would have had the opportunity to tinker with the Standard Heralds, the Ambassadors, and the Fiats where the engine was visible in its discreet pieces. One could easily see the carburetor or the distributor and the spark plugs and it was not unusual for the car owner (or their children) to occasionally open up the spark plugs and clean them to keep the engine operating efficiently. Such opportunities are nonexistent now as the car engines have become much more complicated and it would be nearly impossible to reach into the engine without the correct tools even if the user was courageous enough to overcome the alienation related to fixing a tool personally.

The complexity of tools is also evident in the way in which many gadgets have become smaller in size, integrating many different components into tiny pieces making the entire gadget inaccessible. The matter has become somewhat comical as reported in a 2009 story in the *Popular Science* magazine that manufacturers are battling with the fact that the buttons on a phone have become so small and so crowded together that an average adult finger is too large to operate these devices. The nearly ubiquitous cell phone is an example of the condition where the user would be hard pressed to understand what is inside the phone even if one were to open up the phone.

Miniaturization has been most evident in the case of the microprocessor that makes up the primary component of cell phones, digital music players, computers, and any digital equipment one might be using. There is almost no way to repair a microprocessor that has gone bad. Even if the user is willing to overcome the alienation related to attempting a repair, the user simply might not ever be able to understand what could be wrong with a cell phone that refuses to turn on. The problem could be with the complex microprocessor that simply needs to be replaced and no repair is feasible. That kind of complexity essentially builds alienation and eliminates the possibility of overcoming the alienation from technology. Eventually, even if an individual is willing to overcome the alienation and opens up a complex machinery, they might go through a sufficiently negative experience that they will never attempt the repair again.

IS IT REALLY FIXED?

Users who take on the task of attempting to repair a tool and are able to gain some success with the process still have to be sure if the tool has been repaired properly. This question is an ancillary issue related to answering the question, "Can I fix it?" Even if an affirmative answer was available, it might not be entirely clear if the repair takes care of the entire problem or it only addresses a portion of the problem. I have earlier used examples from medicine, making the point that most medicines and medical procedures are indeed tools and technologies that are meant to address problems with the body. With increasing costs of medical care, there is a tendency to self-medicate where the "tool" that is being repaired, is the human body. Here the notion of alienation can take on deadly outcomes. A person who believes that he or she has overcome the sense of alienation related to medical tools could well decide to self-medicate, or medicate someone else to fix a health problem without fully overcoming the other levels of alienation and understanding fully well how a medical technology, like a medicine, actually works. Consider, for instance, the way in which medicines like antibiotics are used in a rather cavalier way. It is not impossible to obtain the class of drugs that cure a bacterial infection without first going to a doctor, and an individual could use such medicines to treat the symptoms of a cold. If the cold symptoms are the result of a viral infection then the antibacterial medicine would simply be useless to treat the condition because they function by killing the offending bacteria in the case of a bacterial infection.

Unfortunately, these medicines also kill useful bacteria in the body and in the absence of the harmful bacteria these drugs do more harm than good to the body. Such examples point towards a significant issue with the different kinds of alienation discussed here. Those people who feel that they are overcoming the level of alienation related to the repair of tools might actually be fooling themselves into believing that they have actually done an effective repair without knowing if indeed all the necessary functions of a tool have been restored correctly.

One of the reasons that lead to the lack of information about the quality of the repair is a lack of understanding of what exactly was wrong with the tool. The complex gadgets that surround us might show some symptoms of a problem. For instance, a television might suddenly cease working and the user might be completely in the dark as to the problem that manifests in the symptom. It is not uncommon for people to try and fix a problem by archaic means such as hitting the offending machine hard and in some cases the machine might actually start working. The user would then be satisfied that the energetic tap on the television has actually repaired the machine. On the other hand, the real outcome could be much different. If indeed the reason for the malfunction is a loose electrical connection in the machine, the tap might have temporarily corrected the problem, but a loose connection could eventually become a fire hazard and the alienated user simply would have created a risky situation by not knowing that the repair has been ineffective. The problem, of course, begins with the fact that the alienated person did not know what the specific problem was to start with. Not knowing the problem is also related with misjudging the quality of the repair with respect to regaining all the functionalities related to a machine.

A proper repair of a machinery should restore it to conditions where the machine is able to perform all the functions it was originally intended for. Surely age, and related wear of parts, could reduce the longevity of the machine, but the tool must be able to do all the tasks it was meant for. The desired outcome of a repair is a restoration of all the functionalities that were available prior to the problem with the tool. This is best understood in the realm of medical technology too. A person who might have broken a limb, say a foot, would want to be cured to a point where the person regains the complete use of the foot after the cast is removed and the necessary rehabilitation period is over.

A good "repair" is measured by how well a doctor is able to restore the person to a normal life after the treatment is over and how well the person is able to do the same things that the individual could do before the foot was broken and repaired.

The same analogy can be applied to the process of repairing a tool and the repairer must be able to tell if all the functionalities are indeed properly restored after the repair is completed. Meeting this goal requires overcoming several levels of alienation. To begin with, the person must be clear about the functionalities that were available from the machine. If a person never knew that a cell phone can also be used as a video camera then the person would not look for that functionality in a repaired cell phone, even if the repair was done by an expert. The increasing levels of convergence, discussed in earlier chapters, have made it more difficult to overcome this level of functionality since many users of tools are simply unaware of all the possible functions of some of the gadgets that surround us. The focus on function takes on a specific implication when a machine quits working. The process of quitting is evident in the loss of a core function of the machine.

A cell phone that is unable to make calls, a car that does not start in the morning, a refrigerator that does not keep things cool or a lamp that does not light up all represent the loss of the core functions of the respective tool. These are immediately visible to a user who might be completely alienated from the specific technologies, but would certainly notice that something was amiss when the core functions were lost. This is when the repair/replace question comes in and the user might be able to do something, such as slap a television and make it work again, to regain the core function, but the alienated user might not be able to judge if all the other functions are working properly. Even if the person has been able to "fix" the tool, there is no assurance that the person has gained the level of familiarity with the tool that the person can claim that they have actually overcome the alienation related to being able to repair a tool.

Indeed, the process of regaining the core functionality could happen quite accidentally, and such repairs could have far-reaching systemic outcomes that the alienated user might not be able to fathom or predict, often with dire circumstances.

When I was in college at the Indian Institute of Technology and lived in a dormitory in Kharagpur, India it was not uncommon for students to connect a multitude of electrical components ranging from very powerful music systems to table fans to the solitary electrical outlet available in the room. Often, the large number of gadgets would place an undue load on the electrical system and would lead to the burning out of the protective fuse that was meant to avert disaster from an over-loaded system. Being students of engineering, most of us knew how the fuse works. We knew that the fuse was nothing other than a thin piece of wire which would simply melt when its temperature went too high. An overloaded system would lead to the melting of the fuse stopping the flow of electricity and shutting down the gadgets connected to the outlet. This could be avoided by replacing the fuse wire with something that would not melt, like a razor blade. The metal razor blade would almost never melt and everything would be fine. I have seen that solution being used in other places as well where the protective fuse would be replaced by other metal objects to "repair" a system that kept on shutting down because the fuse would always melt. The danger in such a repair is the fact that the melting of the fuse is actually an indication of the much greater problem that there are too many electrical components connected to a system. The melting fuse is a warning that if the number of components is not reduced then the entire system of wiring that allows the flow of electricity is jeopardized and the vital electrical wires could heat up eventually causing an electrical fire with devastating consequences. This exemplifies the condition where the alienated user does a "repair" which provides a quick fix to the problem but actually creates a problem that becomes much more serious and often invisible to the alienated user.

Most tools have become parts of an interconnected set of machines that must work together for the smooth functioning of a technological system. The malfunction of one of the parts could pose a problem to the entire system. Electricity is one of the best examples of the interconnection where the loss of electricity can completely change the way in which a technological system functions. Many parts of the world suffer from a constant deficit of electricity and people and industries have to adjust to the fact that there would be periods of "load shedding" when the overloaded electrical system would need to be shut down for periods of time. Such shut downs affect every form of activity in a social system because things are so interconnected. Many homes have telephones that are dependant on electricity and the loss of electricity would also then shut down the phones and cell phones in case the cell phone battery is not fully charged. This demonstrates the interconnectedness of technology and the user who is interested in overcoming the level of alienation related to the repair of a tool needs to first familiarize oneself with the way in which the specific tool is connected to a larger system of tools. An inappropriate repair could actually end up being disastrous to the entire system and put many people in jeopardy because an alienated user tinkers with tools without a complete understanding of the way the interconnected system operates.

In many ways, overcoming this level of alienation points towards a level of familiarity with technology that is difficult to come by unless the individual has received formal training in understanding specific tools and repairing specific tools. The best analogy comes from the medical discipline. A doctor spends many years understanding the human body and after a lengthy apprenticeship does a doctor gain the expertise to repair an ailing body. It is unsafe to entrust the process of healing to someone who has simply dabbled with medicine and surgery and expect that that person would be able to cure a sick individual. The same principle applies to the repair of tools where the truly alienated person is someone who has overcome all the previous levels of alienation fully and then attempts to overcome the final level of alienation by specializing in the repair of specific machines and gadgets. It is extremely unlikely that a single person will gain the expertise to deal with the malfunction of the numerous gadgets that surround us now. For instance, someone might have worked sufficiently with computers, without necessarily receiving a formal training, so that the person gains enough expertise to be able to effectively repair some components of the computer. The increasing complexity and the interconnectedness of the tools around us make it increasingly difficult to find a person who is the "handyman" who can fix everything.

Gone are the days of the awe-inspiring characters such as Jeeves, the fictitious butler immortalized by P.G. Wodehouse, who could fix everything from the emotional entanglements of the person he served to his master's car. Such people are indeed fictitious now because there is so much more to fix. Given that one is surrounded by tools, there is more that can potentially stop working and each of these tools has become so complex that it is nearly impossible to overcome the alienation related to all the tools. However, our complex technological surrounding is also the reason why there need to be some attempts to overcoming the alienation related to some of the essential tools so that a person can feel some degree of confidence about being able to control one's technological destiny. Complete alienation at this level can lead to a sense of dependence that can sap one's ability and desire to use the new tools that constantly become available and generally allow one to live a slightly better life.

FINDING A FIX

Alienation from technology usually discourages the desire to experiment with new technology. As discussed earlier, it is often the early adopters of technology that help a tool to become popular among the masses. Those who try the tool first usually quickly overcome the early stages of alienation and are able to handle the level of alienation where they gain the confidence to repair the tool to regain its functionalities without having to turn to dealers and expensive replacement options. Gaining this confidence allows such individuals to continue to experiment with new gadgets, and this process in turn often allows new gadgets to become widely popular. The sense of exploration is critical to overcoming the level of alienation related to repairing a tool. It is important to have the curiosity and the confidence to open up an unfamiliar machine and tinkering with its innards. New things often emerge from such processes where someone is attempting to fix a problem and is sometimes able to develop something that is totally new and fixes a problem, not by repairing the problem, but by providing an alternative solution. Those who are able to attain that level of confidence and expertise are really able to overcome the level of alienation related to specific tools.

A good example is obtained in the realm of the development of a specific computer program like Linux. In 1991 the reigning system that operated most PCs was a system called DOS that was marketed by Microsoft Corporation. The company kept careful wraps on the way DOS worked and most users were relatively alienated from the specific ways in which the computer and DOS operated. Some users were able to overcome the levels of alienation and virtually "hack" into the inner workings of the machine to understand how the machine worked and the basic principles of computer programming. These were the un-alienated hackers who discovered two major problems with DOS (and later Windows)—first, it was not an efficient system and it was almost impossible to fix problems with Windows because the actual computer codes that governed the way DOS and Windows operate was a corporate secret. These problems were fixed by the development of a complete new way of controlling computers. The solution emerged from a 21-year-old computer student in the University of Helsinki in Finland, Linus Tovald, who was a self-taught hacker and he started developing a program that would be transparent to all its users and anyone skilled with computers would be able to improve upon the program and make changes to it. This program came to be known as Linux and has proved to be one of the most popular programs that go head-on with Windows in providing a low-cost and easily fixed alternative. One of the main reasons why Linux can be easily fixed is because there is a large degree of openness regarding the way the program works and many people can overcome their alienation because the system encourages them to do so. Often the solution to a technological problem might not lie in fixing the broken tool, but developing a tool that will not break in the way the earlier tool did.

Eventually the person who is able to fix a tool might do so in many different ways with the goal of restoring the entire original function of the tool, with some possible enhancements as well. The un-alienated individual is able to restore the tool with appropriate tools without the help of a professional whose primary job is to repair the specific machine that is broken. A person who has overcome the level of alienation related to repairing tools is also someone who is able to understand how complex tools are connected with each other and how a flaw in one tool could have an impact on many other machines and systems. An inefficient repair could eventually prove disastrous to the entire system. It is particularly difficult to overcome this level of alienation not only because of the way in which machines are transforming, as discussed in this chapter, but also because, to really overcome this alienation, the person must have overcome all the previous levels of alienation. There is an implicit assumption that to be able to fix the thing, it is important to fully appreciate all the details of the object being repaired. That is a level of technological familiarity that is increasingly difficult to attain because of the many different reasons that have been discussed in the previous chapters. One of the significant dangers with the level of alienation related to fixing problems is the fact that those who are alienated at other levels might not even realize that they are alienated and could end up doing things with tools that could be extremely dangerous. There is always a sense of frustration when faced with a tool that does not do what it is expected to, and there is thus a temptation to find a quick fix for the problem. Often, those who are alienated at all the different levels would become impatient and do a dangerous thing just to make the tool do its task, even temporarily. Unfortunately, as machines become complex, and get interconnected, there is nothing 'quick' about repairing things. In a society that has become increasingly "hyper," and demands things "right here, right now," there is a constant tension between doing something right and doing something quickly. There is an old saying among computer repair people that the first mistake that an alienated person makes when repairing computers is assuming it can be done fast. Some repairs could take a lot of time, and alienation from technology often leads to an impatience with technology that can not only be harmful for the person but also actually drive the person further away from the tool—making the person even more alienated.

It is, however, the case that there are different levels of alienation that can be found in any societal system. The next two chapters discuss the ways in which the varying levels of alienation are related to different strengths and weaknesses.

6

I Am Glad I Don't Know

*T*he different levels of alienation discussed so far refer to a hierarchy of alienation where people have different amounts of information about the tools that they use. Generally, most people remain alienated as the machines around us become increasingly complex and interconnected. The issue that becomes important in such a scenario is the way in which people react to these alienations. Usually, as long as people can use their cell phones, televisions, computers, cars, and other machines, there is no need to overcome the alienation because it adds to the burden of using the machines. As demonstrated in the anecdotes, people are usually content with the level of information about the technology that surrounds them and it is relatively difficult to convince people to overcome their alienation. This is especially true since the alienation usually does not seem to hurt people and there is a significant amount of work involved in overcoming the alienation. Indeed, it is difficult enough to juggle the various demands of everyday life, and it becomes onerous to understand how all the machines work, as long as they do what an individual wants the machine to do. It is unimportant to most people to know how a toaster works as long as it makes toasts, and the additional information about the inner workings of a cell phone is just unnecessary information that does not appear to immediately add to the everyday needs of the person.

A consequence of this sense of burden leads to a desire to be alienated where the user can claim that the machines are too complicated and there is no way in which it is possible to know how all the different units work. There is recognition among average users that machines are getting too complicated and in that environment it might be best not to try to understand how things actually work. The complexity of tools leads to a desire to be alienated. Many would argue that it is unimportant to know of all the tools and it is enough to know just the amount needed to do the things required for living a normal life. This tendency can lead to a condition where many people simply reject the tools around them because they are so alienated that they feel no need to learn about the tools. This is a rejection of technology that stems from alienation from specific tools and not because it is something that people are fundamentally opposed to. This is also a condition that is relatively novel because tools have become complicated enough for people to reach a point of being scared to use them simply because they are unable or unwilling to overcome the levels of alienation.

NO NEED FOR THE TOOL

Rejection of technology is not something that is necessarily new, but the reasons of rejection are shifting as machines become more complicated. There are several historical instances of rejecting technology. Most of the reasons have, however, been less connected to the tools and more related to the political and social significance of technology. Consider, for example, the story of the Luddites of the 1800s in England. The early period of the nineteenth century witnessed rapid industrialization in England, Western Europe, and North America. The hall mark of the Industrial Revolution was the transfer of manufacturing from handmade products to mass-produced products in factories that employed thousands of workers who required minimal skills to make the huge machines work. Charlie Chaplin in his famous film *Modern Times* satirized the Industrial Revolution and the related factories by depicting the alienated worker who was literally sucked into the machine and spit out at one end of the giant contraption. The Luddites were opposed to one specific component of the Industrial Revolution—the cotton mills of England. The key argument of the Luddites did not relate to the machines or their alienation from the machines, but they were worried about the loss of work as large factories took over the work of the people who were involved with the non-mechanized textile business of England. Their reason to reject technology was not because they did not understand the technology but they were opposed to the social and economic consequences of adapting technology. Indeed, the Luddites were quite familiar with the technology and were able to enter into factories and destroy key elements in a factory to render it useless. One needs a fair amount of familiarity with the tool to stop it from working and the Luddites were indeed relatively un-alienated, but opposed the tools for what the tools were doing to their way of life. This is a very different form of rejection compared to the way in which the alienated would hesitate using the modern tools.

Similar rejection of technology has also been witnessed in other situations as in the case of British India where the struggle for independence led to a desire to reject the tools that the Indians felt were subjugating them to British rule. Mahatma Gandhi exemplified this in the rejection of the industrialized way of making cloth and salt and encouraged people in India to adopt the traditional spinning wheel and make salt from sea water. While neither of these technologies was eventually adopted as the key way of making cloth or salt in independent India, the rejection of the technology was related to issues that did not necessarily deal with the technology but addressed the political importance of the rejection and the symbol that the technology stood for. Such rejections had little to do with alienation from the technology. Indeed, much like the Luddites, people in India were not alienated from the technologies of subjugation, but were able to understand the technology enough, in order to reject it.

Other examples of technology rejections have almost always represented a very clear understanding of the technology and those who have rejected the tools have done so precisely because they knew how the technology worked and what it could do. A telling example of this comes from the work of Robert Oppenheimer, the architect of the Manhattan Project that resulted in the building of the atomic bombs that were used against Japan in World War II. Although Oppenheimer and other related scientists—no doubt a set of people who were not at all alienated from the technology—were excited with the new invention, they did make an appeal to the American government about not using the bomb because of the devastating consequences of using the technology. Unfortunately the appeal was rejected but the appeal demonstrated a point where a specific technology was being shunned not because people did not know what it could do, but precisely because they knew what it could do, and how it did it.

Most of such historical rejections of technology also occurred at a collective level where large groups of people would demand the rejection. These were instances where people quite familiar with the technology would ask for a societal rejection of the technology because they understood how the technology operates and how the use of the technology could pose some specific political, social, and cultural consequences that were considered to be detrimental to the group of people. In such cases there is little individual decision about rejection and the decision is not based on the level of alienation. Indeed, in some situations the technology itself becomes less critical to the decision to reject it. Consider for instance the amazing leaps made in the area of stem cell research across the world in the early part of the twenty-first century. This research has focused on the use of a special kind of cells called stem cells in the human body that allows scientists to use those cells to generate specific body organs. Part of the stem cell research depends on obtaining the cells from fetuses, and thus the way in which the research is conducted has been associated with the debates related to the ethics and morality of abortion. Different nations and different political groups have different positions on the abortion debate, with the more conservative position being one that rejects stem cell research because of its relation to abortion and the rights to life of the fetus. The American political administration of the early 2000s, under the stewardship of George Bush, was generally opposed to stem cell research not because the scientific advisors to George Bush were alienated from the research, but because there were powerful political lobbies and interest groups opposed to the research. As a result, much of the stem cell research progressed unbridled in the rest of the world, whereas American scientists are finding that they have a significant amount of catching up to do after the political climate in America shifted with the election of Barack Obama as the President. Such rejections of technology happen at the collective level and alienation has little to do with the rejection.

The interesting aspect of the alienation and rejection of technology is the fact that the rejection happens at the personal level where an individual, because of alienation, would reject the tool. It is not a political, cultural or moral motivation that leads to a person declaring that the individual will not use the computer. It is merely a personal choice based on the way the person looks at the tool and is simply intimidated by the technology. The decision to reject a tool is made at the personal level and the user decides that the machine is too complicated and thus not usable or necessary. This only changes when the technology becomes so popular that there is no option other than having to use it. In such situations, there are reluctant users who are unable to overcome their alienation and have to stumble through the process of using the system, that many feel has been imposed on them. Consider, for instance, the way in which a person is forced to use some tools even though the user might remain completely alienated from the way in which the emerging technology of "voice recognition" is being used in the service industry. These systems greet phone callers who are seeking customer support, for instance from the cell phone service provider, with a machine-generated voice requesting the caller to speak out specific responses. If the caller wants to discuss the payment of a bill, the system would ask the caller to say "pay bill," and the system offers such choices. The system then recognizes the spoken words and transfers the call to the correct department, where the caller could be greeted with more such voice recognition systems. Eventually, the caller might never speak to a real human being and might have to navigate through a labyrinth of choices to seek help with the issue the caller might have called about. The major change from the traditional customer service system is the reliance on machines to solve the customer problems and to eliminate the human being from the process at the company's end. Yet, those who are alienated from this technology could get frustrated to the point that they no longer use the tool at all and stop calling customer service phone numbers because the entire process of seeking help could become very frustrating. Ironically, rejection of this technology becomes a personal choice since those who are familiar with the technology are able to use it efficiently. For instance, each requested voice prompt is associated with a key on the telephone number pad. So, it is not essential to speak out anything, but simply punch the corresponding key. In most cases, hitting the number "0" numerous times during the voice prompted system could yield an operator or some other real human being allowing the user to have a conversation with a person as opposed to a machine. It is possible to reject this technology up to a point only, because this method of handling calls placed to a service department of a company is becoming increasingly popular and those who are resisting it could become a small minority who will have to forego customer service assistance if they refuse to use the voice prompts. This is especially true because alienation remains a very personalized process, and unless numerous alienated people come together to reject the same tool, it becomes very difficult to continue to avoid using machines because one is alienated from the technology.

It is only in some situations where an entire block of people would reject a tool because either the tool is not good or it becomes a large number of people who have to overcome the alienation related to the tool as in the case of the infamous digital audio tape player which was introduced in the early 1990s but proved to be such a cumbersome machine that it did not do well in the marketplace leading to its eventual demise. Such events are examples of a large number of people remaining alienated from a technology and eventually rejecting it.

The alienated user also tends to underuse specific tools because the user simply does not know the potential of a machine. Elsewhere I have discussed the "open-ended potential" of technology in saying that there are many ways in which technological developments open up new ways of doing things. The cell phone is an example of a tool that has transformed the way an entire continent of people communicate as in the case of Africa where the traditional landline telephone had a dismal penetration rate with just a small portion of the population having a phone at home, but the cell penetration has been so widespread that people in all strata of society now own cell phones. In other places like in the small towns in India, it is possible to call for a cycle rickshaw by calling the cell phone number of the rickshaw driver just as one would order a taxi in metropolitan areas. There is an urban legend about a rickshaw puller in Calcutta, which still has the notorious and somewhat inhumane human-drawn rickshaw, where the passenger of the rickshaw was lamenting that her cell phone was not working, and the rickshaw puller stops the rickshaw, asks his passenger to dismount, and then brings out a cell phone from under the seat and lets the passenger use it. While such stories might not be true, it does demonstrate the level of penetration of the cell phone in a country like India. Similar stories emerge from parts of Africa, where fishermen would use their cell phones to check market prices of fish before they bring their catch to shore. Such phenomenon reflects the open-ended potential of the cell phone technology. The alienated user, however, often is unable and unwilling to explore the entire range of possibilities offered by a tool. The alienation from the tool becomes a discouragement and the apprehension about the tool leads to the underuse. Eventually, that apprehension becomes habitual and extends from one new tool to another with the alienated user always remaining at the lower end of the use spectrum. Interestingly, many such low-use alienated people would defend their inability to use the tool to its best claiming that the tool is too complicated. The alienated user often would not want to overcome the alienation, but point towards the nature of the technology as the reason for underuse. A simple example is obtained from the cell phone as well. Nearly every cell phone system across the world offers the opportunity to send and receive text messages and in most cases that is something that is relatively simple to do. Yet, in a study conducted in 2005, it was found that in America only 31 percent of the people between 28 and 39 years of age would use the SMS function of the cell phone and only 18 percent of the people between 40 and 49 years of age would use the SMS function on the cell phone. Similar tendencies are true for other parts of the world where the older users of cell phones remain more alienated from the

SMS component of the technology and are thus not being able to use the cell phone to its best advantage. This underuse of tools has become so noticeable that some institutions are beginning to take advantage of the fact that there are numerous PCs that are left turned on and not used for any purpose. An international group called "World Community Grid" invites anyone in the world to donate unused time on the PC to assist in the computation of the complex mathematical problems that would eventually allow for finding solutions for pressing issues such as global warming. The very idea of such a project relies on the alienated user who leaves a PC unused and turned on while connected to the Internet. A certain strange dilemma arises in situations like this since there is no good reason to waste the electricity that is used to power an unused PC. In an age where there is much greater sensitivity to how much energy is being used per person, there are constant reminders that unused machines should be turned off. Yet, large numbers of people do not do that and their participation in the global computing project actually helps solve problems. Indeed, in 2009, there were 400,000 users who were offering their computers to be used during computations. This is a miniscule group in view of the millions of computers that are left on for days and remain unused and idle because the user is not only sufficiently alienated from the machine and simply does not have any use for the machine, but is also afraid to turn it off.

ALIENATION AND TRANSPARENT TECHNOLOGY

As the tools have become more complicated there is an ongoing desire to remain alienated and use that alienation as a point of pride. There are numerous ways in which the alienation has been encouraged and sometimes even rewarded. Consider, for example, a tale that has been distributed over the Internet many times, which describes the life of a poor person who seeks work as a janitor at a technology company. The story says that the man is refused the job because the person does not use e-mail and the dejected person leaves the office crestfallen. However, on his way back home he thinks of a scheme where he is able to set up a simple business buying and selling fruit and eventually becomes wildly wealthy without ever having used e-mail, at which point the person attempts to purchase some life insurance, and the story concludes as follows:

> Planning for the future, he decides to buy some life insurance.
>
> Consulting with an insurance adviser, he picks an insurance plan to fit his new circumstances. Then the adviser asks him for his e-mail address in order to send the final documents electronically.
>
> When the man replies that he doesn't have time to mess with a computer and has no e-mail address, the insurance man is stunned, "What, you don't have e-mail? No computer? No Internet? Just think where you would be today if you'd had all of that five years ago!"
>
> "Ha!" snorts the man. "If I'd had e-mail five years ago I would be sweeping floors at Microsoft and making $5.15 an hour."
>
> Which brings us to the moral: ....
>
> Since you got this story by e-mail, you're probably closer to being a janitor than a millionaire.

Stories like this produce a cultural space where being alienated is not considered to be something that one is necessarily worried about or concerned about. Indeed, a sense of comfort and achievement is tied to alienation, as opposed to the comfort related to overcoming alienation. Indeed, the sense of comfort via alienation is also something that is consciously promoted by the technology industry by the development of tools that can become quickly transparent to the user.

A good example of the process of transparency can be obtained from the way in which people are able to use the Internet. The notion of the Internet as a network of computers emerged from research conducted in the United States by a government agency called the Defense Advanced Research Project Agency (DARPA). In the 1970s, DARPA was asked to help develop a reliable communication tool that would allow key institutions in America to remain connected with each other in the case of a catastrophic event, which in the 1970s was considered to be a nuclear attack from Communist Russia. The research conducted by DARPA and affiliated universities led to the development of a system that allowed computers to connect with each other and exchange information between the connected computers. However, the process of connecting two computers was complicated and it required special skills to be able to establish a successful connection.

Those working with computers in the 1980s would recall the very elaborate process of establishing the connection using a phone and special equipment that would allow sound to carry information from one computer to the other. The equipment to do this would often include a bulky unit that had to be placed next to the computer, and this unit would act as the receptacle for the telephone handset that would rest on the unit and carry the sound, over the telephone wires, to another phone similarly connected to another computer far away. Even with such elaborate connections, the user needed to be sufficiently well-versed with computer programs to change appropriate settings on different operational programs such as the "Winsock" program on PC to enable the two computers to connect properly. After all the trouble of connecting the machines, the information exchanged was typically restricted to texts sent as electronic mail. Using the system that was the prepubescent Internet was certainly not easy and definitely not meant for the alienated.

Within 25 years the situation changed dramatically making it possible for a casual user of a cell phone to easily look at websites that might carry the most recent stock information, or weather forecast. The user just needs to press a couple of buttons on the cell phone key pad to open up the appropriate screen that carries information that is immediately obtained from the Internet. The user might not even realize that the information has arrived from a different computer and was not inherently held in the cell phone. The alienated user has no need to understand from where and how the information is being obtained as long as the information is correct. This represents a level of transparency that allows the user to remain alienated and provides very little incentive to the user to overcome alienation. The tool works as if by magic and the user has to do no more than follow a routine set of steps to be able to do certain tasks with the tool. In the case of the Internet, some of the processes have been made so automated that the user actually has to do nothing other than look at the screen of a cell phone to obtain critical information, such as outside temperature, that the entire process of collecting that information remains transparent to the user. The user does not have to see the steps involved in connecting the cell phone to a centralized computer system that is constantly obtaining weather information from other computer systems and then making the information available to the user. The old days—only 25 years ago—of bulky tools to connect a computer to a phone line have simply disappeared from sight and the technology has become completely transparent. This has been the trend for many new tools where the inner and complex workings of the system have been made transparent to the user of the technology allowing the user to interact very easily with the technology.

Significant amount of research and development has allowed this condition to develop where scientists and technologists have spent large amount of effort in developing systems that can become transparent to the user. A specific yardstick of technological development has been evaluating how transparent the tool is. A very popular set of Web-based tools that emerged around 2005 were websites that allowed people to create communities by connecting with other people. Among these, one that became particularly popular is called "Facebook." Users of this system have to use a computer where they must use a computer program like Internet Explorer to visit the appropriate website and connect with their friends. This involved a specific set of steps where the user had to know how to use the computer, connect it to the Internet, use the correct software to get to the Internet and then open the appropriate website. This is tantamount to telling a user that to turn on a light bulb, one would have to find the fuse box, find a specific switch of the fuse box, turn that switch on and then go to the correct light bulb switch and turn it on. This is a cumbersome process and is certainly not transparent. However, if indeed the user had to take all those steps, the person would be able to overcome some degree of alienation simply because the system was not transparent. New developments, however, make applications like "Facebook" completely transparent. Now anyone can use the "Facebook" application, by flicking the finger across the screen of the iPhone, and be connected to the same network that required the computer and all its ancillary tools. Such transparent tools are similar to the light switch which makes the technology of electricity transparent to the user, increasingly pushing the user further into the zone of alienation as opposed to encouraging the user to overcome the alienation.

The process of transparency is also enhanced by the sense of ubiquity. I discussed the idea of ubiquity to some degree in Chapter 3, but it is useful to see the connection between transparency, ubiquity, and alienation. A technology that has become universally available is often called a ubiquitous technology because it is all around us and we expect it to be available all the time. People become so familiar with ubiquitous tools that these tools only become noticeable when they are not available. Many things that are ubiquitous might not even be sophisticated technologies, but could be systems that people come to expect, and begin to depend on. A public transport system in a large city can be ubiquitous because people who use it simply expect it to be there. An individual going to work in the morning would routinely go to the bus stop, train station or the subway station and know that the transportation will arrive at the time designated on the timetable and the system will transport the person to the destination. Such a system is taken for granted and if the busses stop plying, or the subway system stops people suddenly take note of it and might be led to ask the question, "What went wrong?" This is the moment when the alienated user suddenly becomes aware of alienation and realizes that it might be impossible to answer the question because the person has no idea how the system works and is completely alienated from the system that one relies upon. This is precisely the condition I described in the beginning of the book when describing the process of "being on hold" while circling in a commercial aircraft over a busy airport. Moments such as those remind people that they are getting alienated from a large system, that has technological components, and when the system breaks down there is little recourse left for the alienated user of the system.

The matter becomes even more tantalizing when the ubiquitous system or technology also becomes transparent, and the user not only relies on the tool, but the tool might completely recede from sight and the user might not even realize that there is a technological system at work. To many designers of tools and technological systems the measure of the success of a tool is both its ubiquity and its transparence. A tool that fulfills both these conditions can be considered to be an ideal tool because it eliminates the need for the user to consciously think about the tool or its existence. The way in which the television technology has developed in developed and developing countries illustrates this point well. I recall the days when the television technology was introduced in India in the 1970s. The broadcasts came from the metropolitan television stations and households with televisions required a powerful antenna to receive the signal. Within a few years many homes had televisions and that was evident by the presence of the unique looking television antenna. There was a novelty to the tool and there was the constant tinkering of the direction of the antenna to obtain the best signal. I thought that my father spent more time on the roof adjusting the antenna than actually watching the signal on television! This was certainly not a ubiquitous technology and was far from transparent because every time a sparrow would alight on the television antenna the signal would change and my father would be up on the roof adjusting the system. Within about 20 years, the system changed dramatically in India. In the late 1980s, there was the rampant development of cable television and the antenna was replaced by ungainly cables running between homes carrying the television signal. The poor sparrows suddenly lost the resting place they had become accustomed to as the unsightly antennas were torn down and sold off as scrap metal. The television itself was also more sophisticated, and new machines with remote controls became commonplace. All one had to do was flick the switch on the remote control and a perfect picture would greet the viewer. Watching television did not require constant trips to the roof to adjust the antenna. This process made the technology both ubiquitous and transparent—it was expected to be there and it did not come in the way. It also made the user much less aware of how the technology worked. As new systems were developed there was less information about the way in which the additions worked as long as the experience of watching television was enhanced. Thus, there developed the cable box that users also became used to, and that tool became ubiquitous and transparent as it brought numerous channels to the television screen. There was greater degree of alienation from the technology and the user was unworried and the technology developers were pleased as they developed systems that made the tools even more ubiquitous and transparent.

The relationship between ubiquity and alienation becomes especially important as we are surrounded by a larger number of gadgets and machines that all play an important role in our lives. It is also increasingly the case that more people have access to more machines and gadgets. Traditional indicators of technology ownership have shifted as more tools have entered the social space. It is not uncommon to see people who could be considered to be of a lower income level own gadgets such as cell phones. In countries like India, there is a concerted effort to overcome income as a barrier to technology ownership. For instance, the Tata automobile company in India started manufacturing a car in 2009 that has been described by Tata as the "people's car" and would be available for about $2,500. That could well make it the cheapest car in the world and would help to make it immensely popular in many markets. Such moves, along with the development of inexpensive computers like the Sakshat digital device that was unveiled in 2009 by the University of Andhra Pradesh in India, is making technology quickly accessible to a large cross-section of people in traditionally poorer countries. The computer would sell for a low price which would make it available to a large section of users in India, and possibly also across the world. Such moves help to make technology ubiquitous in different parts of the world, and many of the barriers related to affordability, geography and technical know-how begin to crumble as more people gain access to complex technology.

While there is a continuing drive in some parts of the world to make technology easily available to the masses, private corporations that do global business are also recognizing that there are large groups of people, or markets, that can be tapped to maximize profit by selling new technology in these markets. Yet, the key to that large-scale selling is only possible if the technology can be presented as a transparent tool which is about to become ubiquitous and not owning the technology would place the nonuser in an inherently negative position.

As far as the companies are concerned, the user can remain completely alienated from the technology as long as they are willing to let the technology become ubiquitous and necessary for their everyday life activities. As discussed in Chapter 2, this is precisely the way in which the Palm Pilot became a staple tool for professionals across the world. It did not matter if the user was clear about the way in which the tool worked, as long as they were willing to use it.

The balance between ubiquity, transparency, and alienation was tipped in favor of ubiquity by the experts who designed new technology as well. It was clear to the designer and seller of tools that the success in the marketplace is connected with transparency and ubiquity and not with a tool that opens its innards to the user. This is based on a fundamental presumption that most users are happy to declare, "I am glad I don't know." This becomes the mantra of the designer who is charged with developing a tool that the user can use without ever understanding how it works, as long as the tool does what the user expects it to do. In many ways, the ideal customer is the one who would not ask too many questions about how the tool works, and the designers increasingly moved to a point where the specifics of the way in which the tool works was kept hidden from the user through specific design innovations that would put specific "shells" on tools that would keep the user shielded from the way in which the tool worked. An interesting example comes from the ubiquitous cell phone technology. As the cell phone has become popular, there have also been developments in technology that have led to the development of tools called "smart phones" and "pocket personal computers," that are very sophisticated cell phones that have enhanced computing capabilities. In the early days of smart phones, using most of the phones required some knowledge of the logic that governs the way in which computer programs operate. For instance, a user needed to know that computers often have a hierarchical system for storing digital files which are usually placed in folders and sub-folders. Users of smart phones sold in the early 2000s would need to have rudimentary understanding of such basic computer facts. A completely alienated user would become quickly frustrated with such systems, and the technology would not become ubiquitous mainly because it was not transparent to the user. This was a barrier to the sale of such tools, and companies put in significant effort in the development of smart phones that would be suitable for the alienated user. The iPhone made by Apple Computer was the first significant move in that direction, where a corporation purposefully built a tool that would be particularly attractive to alienated users, who do not want to do anything more than flick their finger on the screen to perform a series of essential tasks. Other companies such as HTC and Samsung quickly followed with their versions of similar tools where the user would be presented with an interface that would be easy to use, and virtually transparent, so that the user never felt intimidated by the tool and could continue to remain alienated. The technology industry constantly fed the desire on the part of the user to remain alienated and new tools are rewarded because they quickly become ubiquitous and disappear from sight and blend in with the 'normal' activities of the person.

THE WILLING USER

This process of creating ubiquitous technology can only be done as long as the user has no difficulties with remaining alienated. The user who wants to overcome alienation at any of the levels suggested here is essentially calling into question what has become normal and conventional. Such inquiries are inherently threatening to a societal and corporate system that relies on the alienation to design and market its products. This tendency extends to many realms beyond technology. The notion of ubiquity and acquiescence to alienation is the hallmark of the idea of hegemony. The hegemonic process is one where people willingly agree to a way of life. Writing about the idea of hegemony in Italy during World War II, Antonio Gramsci[22] suggested that specific groups of people, such as the Italian Fascists, are able to come to power and retain power through a hegemonic process where the people willingly and unquestioningly agree to the way in which social, cultural, and political policies are made and implemented. Those who hold power through a hegemonic process rely on the willingness of a large group to willingly accept the conventional way of doing things. Picking up on Gramsci's ideas, Louis Althusser, a French scholar, argued that there are specific "apparatuses" such as the family and school that operate in a social system that propagates the hegemonic position and allows the powerful to retain power while most people become subjects to that power.[23] Thus, traditionally, families have taught specific gender roles with boys and girls having different expectations. There is no specific reason for the differences except that the family has operated as an apparatus that helps to maintain a hegemonic system of gender differentiation.

A similar process is at work with the technological hegemony that is propagated by corporations that are happy to keep the user in the dark about the way in which things work. Such attempts are successful only because the user is willing to remain in the state of alienation and does not feel the need to understand and then question the way in which technology is being introduced in their lives. The conventional position that ubiquity and transparency promote is one of technological promise where there is an assumption that the new tools would necessarily improve life. The hegemonic process is successful precisely because most people are willing to accept that promise. To be sure, most people are so alienated that it is impossible for them to accept any alternative to the promise. It is only when people begin to overcome the sense of alienation is there a recognition of the unevenness of the promise, and the un-alienated user is in a position to question the hegemonic ubiquity and transparency of tools. This is what leads to the critical consumption of the tool rather than the alienated acceptance of the tool just because it has been promised to do wonders.

What is especially interesting about the condition of alienation is that the alienated user ends up behaving in the same way as a person who believes in the value of technology because of their understanding of the tool and their faith in technology. Some thinkers have suggested that many developments in technology are driven by the fact that many believe in an intrinsic value of technology. This is the kind of thinking that would argue that one should use a tool just because it is available, and because there is a faith that the tool will be good for the user. This mode of thinking has been around for a long time, where specific tools were simply adopted because it was available and those in a position to make decisions erred on the side of technology because they believed that the tool would add value. For example, the adoption of computers in the education sector has been driven by this thinking where many policy makers, who were well-versed in technology and not at all alienated, agreed that computers would "obviously" improve the educational experience. Their enthusiasm for the adoption of technology was precisely because they were not alienated, but were believers in the technology they understood very well. Yet, the alienated user behaves in similar ways precisely because they are alienated and do not want to take the risk of missing what might be promised by a specific tool. Paradoxically, the alienated user and the non-alienated user might appear to behave in exactly the same way but for completely different reasons. This phenomenon is important to note because it is sometimes difficult to definitely understand if someone is using a tool because of hegemonic pressures or because they have overcome their alienation so well that they have become very efficient users of the tool.

This conundrum creates an interesting new way of classifying people in a societal system. Unlike many other hierarchies based on attributes such as gender and race, this new classification is based on the level of alienation from technology which has never been formally measured. There are imprecise tools to measure questionable attributes such as intelligence as in the case of the often debated Intelligence Quotient (IQ) tests, but it is relatively difficult to measure the level of technology alienation. From the behavioral aspect, the alienated and non-alienated user might appear quite similar and it would take sufficient careful observation under different circumstances to establish the level of alienation of a person. Yet, this level has many consequences as discussed earlier in the book. One of the most important of these consequences arises from the way in which the truly un-alienated can utilize the tools that surround us to wield powers that can control the lives of the numerous alienated people. The next chapter examines the way in which the un-alienated become incredibly powerful in a world populated by people working with alien technologies.

7

Those Who Know
Are in Control

*O*ne of the most horrendous acts of terrorism in the twenty-first century was the attack on the Twin Towers of the World Trade Center in New York on September 11, 2001. As most readers would know, the attack was carried out by ramming two passenger airplanes into each tower. As a result, nearly 3,500 lives were lost and the two towers collapsed to the ground, forever changing the skyline of Manhattan Island that made up one of the most best recognized geographic icons in the world. There was a set of very careful examinations of the event from forensic and scientific perspectives to answer the question, "Why did the towers collapse?"

This question becomes especially important because the engineers who designed the towers, and the way the towers were built, had taken into consideration events such as the impact from a plane. However, the scientists and engineers who worked on the question of the collapse after the September 11 event suggested that the towers collapsed because the planes destroyed some of the load-bearing metal pillars that held up the towers, and the intense heat generated by the burning jet fuel weakened the metal pillars that were not destroyed by the impact making the entire structure unstable. The amount of heat was directly related to the amount of jet fuel that the planes were carrying. The two planes that were used for the attack had both been fueled up to make the 3,000-mile flight from the east coast of the United States to its west coast and the planes were completely loaded with the fuel all of which burned after the planes hit the towers. Naturally, if the planes were smaller aircrafts doing regional flights with lesser fuel then the heat generated might not have been sufficient to lead to the catastrophic collapse. The various governmental and nongovernmental bodies that examined the attack agreed that the terrorists carefully chose which flights to hijack and use for the attack. The flights were selected to ensure that there would be sufficient fuel to create the heat that could eventually lead to sufficient softening of the metal to lead to the collapse. What remains striking about the way in which the attack happened and its planning is the elaborate levels of training and understanding of the technology of the building and the tools used for the attack that were demonstrated by the terrorists. As investigations revealed after the attack, the terrorists were not only indoctrinated into a specific brand of religion but also had learnt the different ways in which the building could be attacked to cause maximum harm. Technologically, these were people who were not at all alienated from the tools they used. From the days of hiding in San Diego to the final selection of the flights to hijack for the attack, these terrorists demonstrated that they had overcome different levels of alienation with relation to technology. Far before the attacks, the terrorists understood how telephone systems worked in the United States and restricted their phone conversations to public phone booths to avoid attention on the residential phone numbers of the apartments where they lived, the terrorists also knew the different ways of transferring money between different countries and understood which were undetectable tools to do transfers as opposed to the methods that could give them away. In a very chilling way the 9/11 attackers demonstrated that they had been able to overcome some of the alienations from technology that many people would not even dream about. Yet, these dealt with tools that surround all of us and we are often alienated and thus become vulnerable.

Similar stories can be traced to the way in which the terrorists who attacked Mumbai in 2008 used everyday tools to plan and carry out the attack. Numerous commentators have remarked on the way in which the young men who stealthily entered Mumbai were equipped with tools that are easily available commercially, but these terrorists were particularly adept at using the tools in a way that they could keep the security forces eluded long enough to kill nearly 200 people. What is especially telling about the scenario in Mumbai, and in other terrorist instances in India, is the chilling alienation of the everyday security forces in India who are simply incapable of understanding and thwarting terrorist attacks because there is a lack of understanding of the tools that the terrorists could be using. Consider, for instance, one of the ways in which the evil-doers were able to use the ubiquitous wireless Internet technology to hide from the authority and still continue to stay in touch with their network. This use of the Internet carries over to other criminals who are able to take advantage of the alienated users of the transparent technology to gain control on Internet resources. Consider, for instance, the way in which the well-known wireless Internet technology has become vulnerable in the hands of the alienated user. Over the past few years there has been a rapid adoption of wireless Internet tools in many homes where the home owner would create a wireless zone in the home so that a laptop computer could be used anywhere in the house without having to plug it into a wired Internet outlet. These zones are known as Wi-Fi networks and multiple machines, including smartphones, could be connected to these networks. In the commercial version of such Wi-Fi systems most network administrators are trained to design the zones in such a way that only authorized users with appropriate passwords would be able to use the network. On the other hand, many alienated users would set up a zone in a home or a small business like a coffee shop by following the simple instructions that are provided with the tools required to set up the system. The alienated user often fails to put in the protection that is needed to prevent unauthorized use of the wireless zone. Those who know that alienated users often fail to set up the protection take advantage of the weakness, and one could simply stand outside a private home and be connected to the Internet with a smartphone without anyone even realizing that a complete stranger has just hijacked a Wi-Fi connection to send and receive e-mail messages, or even make phone calls over the Internet. The alienated user becomes an accomplice in a criminal act without even realizing how they are helping those who are not alienated.

ALIENATION AND POWER

Being alienated from technology is closely connected to the way in which power is distributed in a social system as well. Traditional power has been connected with elements such as political, cultural, economic, and military clout with the powerful being the people who have controlled and defined what is acceptable within a social structure which could be as microscopic as a neighborhood under the control of a goon to a global system of power distribution with some countries, enjoying the advantage of a superior and better funded military, being able to shape global policy. These are conditions where power is connected to having an advantage in some specific element and using that advantage to manipulate those who are less fortunate. The connection between power and alienation from technology occurs in somewhat the same way.

Those who are alienated from technology become powerless because they are unaccustomed with the way in which much of the technological world operates around them. This alienation by itself might not be tremendously troublesome and the alienated could perhaps muddle their way through the technological labyrinth without causing any major harm to themselves and to others. The corporations who produce the technology would continue to provide the support that the alienated would need to survive in the increasingly technological world. The matter becomes somewhat more complicated when those who have overcome alienation also recognize how helpless the alienated are with the technologies that everyone is compelled to use. The powerlessness of the alienated becomes manifest when the small number that have overcome alienation are able to utilize the ignorance of the alienated to begin to take advantage of the alienated masses.

Coercive power has almost always been exercised by recognizing that someone is powerless because of a deficiency. In its raw form, a person with a gun is automatically powerful over an obviously unarmed person, because the one with the gun sees that the victim does not have the gun. This knowledge becomes the source of power. On the other hand if the armed person suspects that the victim could also be armed that would give a pause before one would try to overpower the other. This logic applies to the issue of the power dynamics based on different levels of alienation. Those who have overcome alienation not only understand how a technological system works but also are able to quickly gather if someone else is alienated. Those who are alienated from technology are often unable to recognize the weak points of the tool and become vulnerable because of that. The situation of setting up Wi-Fi at home is a good example of the process where the alienated is simply unaware of the dangers associated with connecting a home computer to the Internet without putting into place adequate measures to protect the data that is contained on the home computer.

This weakness can not only be used by terrorists to plan attacks but also is a weakness that can be used by a criminal intent on stealing private and personal information contained on the home computer.

Starting in the early 2000s one of the largest criminal activities in the developed countries has been identity theft where personal information is illegally obtained and used. In 2008 there were nearly 10 million people in America who were victims of identity theft. The process of identity theft includes someone collecting personal information about another individual and then using that information to impersonate the victim and to begin making financial transactions while taking on the identity of the victim. Such an activity would start with collecting personal identification numbers that are tied to the financial and personal records. For example, many countries use some kind of a national numbering system where every legal citizen of a nation has a unique number assigned to the person which ties the individual with important information such as financial records, bank information, and even welfare information related to what amount of support the individual might get from the state. For instance, in India, after independence, the government set up a system where every individual was issued a "ration card" which allowed the individual to purchase subsidized food from government stores. Although the system was relatively "low tech," using a paper card and a process of check marks to indicate weekly use, people very quickly found ways of abusing the system to obtain more than what they were supposed to receive as ration. A similar system exists in America, where people with lower income are eligible for food stamps that allow them to purchase food from stores using the stamps as opposed to money. These systems all rely on personal information that should remain private to protect the person. Before the advent of digital tools, much of this information was stored in paper ledgers which were often carefully kept behind locked doors. The adoption of digital tools has led to a condition where a significant portion of the personal information is kept as computer records which can become vulnerable unless the information is appropriately protected.

The paradox with the personal information on computers is the fact that the computer system offers a far more robust process of protection than any physical lock and key could. Mathematicians and computer scientists have come up with numerous ways of encrypting data ensuring that it would take a stroke of luck for a thief to be able to access the data. The simplest means of data protection is the use of a password to restrict access to a computer.

Most computer systems would require a password to access all the information that is stored on the computer's hard drive. For instance, a person might keep sensitive information related to bank accounts using popular financial software. Some of these financial computer programs would contain all the numbers required for a thief to quickly access the funds. Distributors of these computer programs urge users to protect the data with passwords. Unfortunately, many who are alienated from technological systems do not fully understand the importance of the passwords and often either do not use a password or do not use one that offers any protection. Some studies have revealed that many alienated users would use passwords that are easy to guess, with the digits "123456" being used by numerous users. An investigation by the British Broadcasting Corporation (BBC) revealed in 2004 that nearly a third of computer users would use a password that was based on the name of a child or a pet, and many would write down their passwords making it easily available to others. Those who are out to do mischief can access these passwords or guess the information to be able to get access to sensitive information. This process has become even more dangerous because of the Internet which offers opportunities to buy things online as well as do financial transactions using the Web. Those who are aware of the habits of the alienated users can take advantage of the alienation and dupe users into revealing sensitive information.

The early part of the twenty-first century saw the growth of unscrupulous users who would set up fake websites that would mimic the look of legitimate businesses and services and invite the alienated user to reveal personal information. This method, often called "phishing," leads the alienated user to a website that looks authentic where the user would enter in names, phone numbers, personal identification numbers, and even credit card numbers. This method works only because users who are alienated from the system do not take the trouble to check the legitimacy of websites before revealing information. Those users who are less alienated are often more careful about the ways in which they use the Internet and are able to protect themselves better. Eventually an uneasy power relationship develops between the alienated user and the ones who are able to overcome the alienation. The alienated could be taken advantage of in many different ways where an alienated individual might not at all be aware that someone else is using their lack of understanding of the technology to a point where the alienated user could actually be harmed by those who are abusing their alienation. These situations can be as simple as being convinced by the technological jargon that salespersons might use to sell a new technology promising many things that the alienated user would have no understanding of, but would be persuaded to purchase. At the same time, the process of alienation could lead to a point where the user could be simply helpless in the face of assault by those who are not alienated and the hapless user could have one's life destroyed.

One of the key components of the power relationship that develops between the alienated user and those who are not alienated is the way in which the alienated user can be taken advantage of without the person ever realizing what is happening to them. Being alienated makes people unaware of the power of some tools that surround them and how those tools could be used against the alienated people. In some situations the power would be wielded by legitimate organizations who fully know that the user is alienated and thus oblivious to what the tools are doing to them. George Orwell's classic futuristic novel—*1984*—made this point in describing a social system where the oppressive state apparatus was able to create a condition where every move of every individual would be observed and judged by the faceless "big brother" who is omnipresent via tools that surround the population. At least in the case of George Orwell's novel, most people in the population knew they were alienated from the tools and knew that they were being observed. The situation is quite different in reality in 2008 when many people are actually so alienated that they are not even aware of how certain institutions are utilizing the popular alienation to keep track of people. In these cases the alienation automatically places large groups of people in a subordinate power position because they simply do not understand the power of the tools that surround them and thus become subjects to those who understand and control the tools.

The process of taking advantage of popular alienation is evident in a practice that has become commonplace with many retail stores across the world that provide a "loyalty card." Large chains of grocery stores in the West would offer these cards that are issued to a customer after the customer provides personal information. Possession of the card allows customers to take advantage of special sales offers from the stores. Other stores would offer cards where a customer is given a free gift after making a certain number of purchases or spending a certain amount of money. What is interesting to note is the way in which these schemes work. All that the customer has to do when buying at a store like Shopper's Stop or Macy's is to give the salesperson the card and it contains all the necessary information to update the customer's account which is saved on a central computer. The customer might not even realize where the information is kept and how it might eventually be used. The alienated customer is usually completely unaware of the way in which the data is maintained and used, and some might even be alienated from the fact that the data is indeed being stored and used. Usually, the customer is happy to receive the promised discount or free gift. The technological system, however, is geared to keep track of the person's buying habits and demographics and even sell that information to other merchants who would want to entice the individual to buy other products. This process provides those who know how to use the data a sense of power and control over the alienated people who are willingly giving up personal information without considering the way in which the information could be used. What is especially interesting to note about the way in which corporations collect and use information is that all of the data is voluntarily provided by the customer. There is very little deception in these processes, and the customer would often sign a "Terms of Condition" statement when completing the personal information form. Unfortunately, much of this is done in a state of alienation from the specific process as well as the technological system that will be eventually used to manage the data. In being alienated, and thus by not asking the required questions, the customer is willingly giving up personal information and placing the corporations in a position of power. A futuristic tale helps to make the point:

Pizza man: "Thank you for calling Pizza Hut. Can I have your …"

Customer: "Hi, I want to order something."

P: "Can I get your National ID Number?"

C: "My National ID Number, yeah, wait, that's 6102049998-45-54610."

P: "Thank you, Mr Schwardt. You live at 25 Rose Street and your telephone number is 89 568 345. Your company number on Alliance Street is 74 523 032 and your extension is -56. But you are using your cell phone now, where are you calling from?"

C:	"Huh? I'm at home. Where did you get all this information from?"
P:	"We are connected to the system."
C:	(sighs) "Oh, of course. I will have two of your specialty pizzas with a lot of meat."
P:	"I do not think it's good for you."
C:	"What ??!!"
P:	"According to your medical records you have high blood pressure and high cholesterol. Your health insurance would not allow unhealthy choice."
C:	"Damn, what do you recommend then?"
P:	"You could try our soy yogurt pizza with very little fat. You will certainly like it."
C:	"How come that I might like it?"
P:	"Well, last week you borrowed the book 'Healthy Gourmet' from the library. That's why I recommended you this pizza."
C:	"Ok, ok. Give me two of them in family size. How much are they?"
P:	"That should be for you, your wife and your four children. The cost would be 45 Euros."
C:	"Here is my credit card number."
P:	"I'm sorry, but you will have to pay in cash. You have reached your credit limit on the credit card."
C:	"I will walk down to the cash machine and get cash before your driver is here."
P:	"That might be difficult because your account is overdrawn."
C:	"No matter. Just send the pizzas. I will have the money. How long will it take?"
P:	"We are a little behind. It is about 45 minutes. If you are in a hurry, you can pick up after you obtain the money, although the transportation

	of pizzas on a motorcycle is always a little difficult."
C:	"How do you know that I ride motorcycles?"
P:	"Here it says that your car was taken back by the bank because you did not pay the loan, but your motorcycle is paid for, so I will assume that you are using."
C:	"@#%/$@§?#!"
P:	"Be careful about how you speak. We note that in July 2006 you were arrested for being abusive and insulting people."
C:	(speechless).
P:	"Would you like to order the pizza?"
C:	"Yes. Oh, but please do not forget the two free liters of Coke, which according to your advertising, come free with the pizza."
P:	"I'm sorry, but the exclusion clause prohibits us from sending free soft drinks to people with diabetes."

This, hopefully unlikely, and somewhat amusing, story has been circulating on the Internet and is based on a video produced by a human rights activist group called the American Civil Liberties Union which warns people of a scary future where all the information about an individual is centralized and available to multiple organizations. These organizations could automatically gain control on the alienated and powerless individual who might not even know how much personal information might be stored on interconnected computer systems.

BEING POWERLESS

The process of alienation can make people powerless by creating a large group of individuals who lose their power because they are unaware of the way in which technological systems could be used to control one's life. While corporations are interested in collecting information about the way in which a person might choose to spend money, other special computer systems keep track of the credit-worthiness of a person as in the case of credit scoring systems developed in most countries which use different pieces of data to do a statistical calculation helping to predict the likelihood that a person will repay a debt. The mathematical and technological system that operates this system is kept a secret, hence, automatically alienating an individual. In such situations, a person wanting to overcome the alienation remains helpless because the law disallows the possibility of obtaining the answers required to overcome alienation. In many cases, the combination of alienation and not being allowed to overcome alienation automatically puts people in a position of weakness.

This powerlessness is most evident when a ruling state would employ technological systems to keep track of their population. In Chapter 3, I briefly mentioned the use of surveillance cameras that can be placed surreptitiously to keep an eye on a specific zone. These have been used in many shops to keep an eye on potential shoplifters, but the use of such cameras has also been widely adopted by governments where it is used as a law enforcement tool. The cameras tend to show up in many public places and people might be completely unaware of the existence of the cameras which could be constantly capturing their activities. The alienation occurs from the dual condition of not knowing that a person is being observed and from the fact that the person has no way of finding out how the information is being used. In some countries the matter has gone to the level where the country has earned a pejorative nickname for the rampant use of cameras that constantly keep track of people, creating a class of people who are powerless in the face of the use of technology. This is especially true for Britain, which has earned the nickname "surveillance society" based on a 2006 report from the BBC that claimed that Britain had nearly 4.2 million cameras operated by the police and other organizations. In other words, there was a camera for every 14 persons in Britain. Most of the people did not even know that they were constantly being observed because a good portion of the cameras were hidden from sight and the population remained largely alienated from the tool. Yet, those who have access to the information being gathered by these tools can gain significant power over the alienated people who are subjects to the tool. Sometimes the power can be used in a beneficial way. Consider the story that appeared in the Calcutta newspaper called *The Telegraph* on June 3, 2008 that reported that the police were able to apprehend a couple of thieves who had used stolen bank cards to withdraw money from cash machines. The thieves, alienated from the fact that cash machines use surveillance cameras, did not realize that their faces were being captured by the cameras, and the police was able to catch them by distributing the pictures. There are many other instances where surveillance cameras have been useful in catching criminals who were alienated from the way in which the technology worked and thus made mistakes that lead to the capture. The matter becomes different when a state is in the position to exercise power over the law abiding people as a part of the process of improving security in the face of unknown attackers such as the ones who created havoc in the hotels in Mumbai in 2008. The threat of attack offers the rationale to employ technological systems that work invisibly to keep track of people who are always necessarily alienated from the tools and technologies.

One of the key components of the powerlessness that is produced by alienation is the way in which a system made up of technologies and bureaucracies attempts to contain the information that one would require to overcome alienation. In most cases, as discussed in this book, alienation can be partly attributed to individuals who are willing to remain alienated and are not worried by the fact that they do not know what is going on around them. This condition is desirable for those who want to retain a sense of power over the alienated, and there is little attempt to help people overcome the alienation. In other words, governments that have set up millions of surveillance cameras do not suddenly become interested in explaining to the population how the cameras work and how the information is used. There is an implicit "do not ask - do not know" policy that operates where people eventually become accustomed to cameras facing them and most people learn to live with the alien technology as long as it remains unobtrusive and does not appear to interfere with the everyday life of people.

The situation becomes different when an individual or a group of people begin to notice that the fact that they are alienated from some technological systems seems to be making them more vulnerable, and at that point they want to know how the technological system works. There is then a genuine desire to overcome alienation and be able to use the system in a more efficient manner. However, the power relationships that become conventionalized based on alienation are maintained by withholding information from the alienated, thus not allowing them to become powerful by gaining the expertise needed to work with a technological system. Some of the best examples of this process come from corporate systems which would keep certain components of a tool completely hidden from the user so that the user continues to remain powerless. Examples of this process are also evident with governmental systems that would refuse to divulge information in an attempt to keep the people alienated. Usually the process unfolds with statements that remind the individual that they are indeed alienated, and they would be unable to understand the complexity of a technological system and it is best not to ask about the complex system.

The phenomenon of assuming that a person is alienated is most often evident in areas where there is a persistent culture of expertise. This is a condition where some can claim expertise because of specialized training and the experts necessarily assume that those who are not trained are surely alienated. This is especially evident within the medical profession where the physician, or those trained in the profession, would often treat the "common" alienated people in a manner where details of medical procedures might not be clarified to a patient or a patient's family simply because the trained professionals assume that the alienated commoner would not understand what the treatment is about. This becomes particularly critical when the treatment has a technological component and the medical professionals would simply not explain the technology because there is an assumption that the alienated persons would not understand it. The alienated might also actually assume that the technology is extremely complicated and voluntarily become powerless in the face of the expertise that the 'professional' offers. This is where the sense of alienation is specially debilitating because an individual might be reminded that it is impossible for the person to grasp the complexity of the medical technology, and is expected to simply rely on the un-alienated expert who knows the tools.

With the growing presence of tools in many different segments of everyday life, the tendency to assume that many people are alienated begins to permeate to many different aspects of life beyond medical treatment. The assumptions of alienation show up in the computer industry as more people are gaining access to computers, and are consequently requiring support with their machines. These are people who could well be alienated from the tools they use, and the experts that they have to turn to would often assume that the help-seeker is indeed alienated and consequently offer to help in a way where the alienated user remains powerless and reliant on the expert. There is little motivation on the part of the expert to provide any information that would actually reduce the alienation of the person they are supposed to be helping. The alienated remain powerless because of all the reasons discussed in this book, and are unable to even begin to ask appropriate questions. There is thus a vicious cycle where those in the know continue to perpetuate the culture of expertise and those who are alienated continue to remain in that condition, and get pushed further away from the technology they are compelled to use. This process becomes evident, for instance, in the following advertisements for technology help:

> Dynamic computers provides product of desktop computer solutions, server solutions, peripheral solutions, power devices solutions, networking solutions, software solutions, system restoration, etc. (From an advertisement in India.)

> We can virtually connect to your computer to help troubleshoot virtually anything software related. With a limited hardware analysis as well. We offer the latest anti-spyware, anti-virus, and cleanup tools that are available today. Once you have had an initial diagnostics from one of our professionals we provide top notch support and tune-up's. These are some other services we have to offer *Network Support *Printer Support *iPod Support *Backup assistance/Data Backup *Spyware and Virus Removal *Windows XP/Vista Support & Training *Digital Camera Setup *New PC Setup *PC optimization. (From an advertisement in America.)

> Solutions for a range of requirements including: PC Repair/ Upgrades/New system supply, IT Equipment sales, Storage, Backup & Recovery, Networking/IT Infrastructure, Website Design and Delivery, Small Business Startup Pack, Internet Wireless & Wired Installation/Health Checks, Disaster Recovery.

> We pride ourselves in delivering honest, expert levels of service with putting our clients and their expectations first. We're Microsoft Professional and Cisco CCNA Accredited to ensure an expert level of service is maintained throughout our business. (From an advertisement in England.)

There is something uncannily similar about the three advertisements that represent numerous others that pop up when doing a Web-based search for information about computer repair. There is a common theme of solving and troubleshooting, which necessarily assumes that there is a problem to be solved. The idea that a computer that is malfunctioning poses a problem suggests that the computer must be an integral part of everyday life and any time the computer does not do what it is supposed to do, it poses a problem. The notion of the 'problem' further assumes that the user of the computer will indeed consider this to be a problem because they are powerless to deal with the malfunction. Implicitly, the powerlessness is the product of alienation where the user is so alienated from the tool that the user would automatically seek the help of the expert who has the power to solve the problem. All three of these advertisements clearly mark out the boundaries of power, which are then connected to the notion of expertise.

Two of the advertisements actually use the terms "expert" and "professional" in the copy of the advertisement, whereas the one from India does not mention that word, but it is assumed that anyone who could provide the solutions has to be more of an expert than the alienated and hapless user. This is a deliberate strategy to sell a service which is principally based on the notion of alienation—one would not be an expert unless the others are alienated and unless the others choose to remain alienated. Interestingly, the people who might be looking at these advertisements and seeking the service have actually accepted their alienation and have voluntarily decided that they are powerless to solve the problem they are facing. In doing that they have further alienated themselves from the tools they are compelled to use. The experts, through their discourse in advertisements, continue to reinforce the alienation by the use of another tool of power—jargon. The advertisements use a specific kind of language that they assume would appear unfamiliar, as most jargon is, to the alienated people.

Most professional groups have a common vocabulary that allows members of the group to communicate in an efficient manner. Such vocabularies have special terms to describe complex situations, and the specialized words allow people to convey complex ideas without having to resort to a large number of words. Some of the words can actually be part of a large range of words and the key word communicates the entire idea. These words are learnt in many different ways. In some professions the terms are learnt through a process of apprenticeship, where a person would work with an experienced person and learn the key words. This mode of learning is particularly true among groups who have a history of working within the same profession for generations. The language is often handed down from parents to children who would do more or less the same specialized activity. This is a form of experiential education where a person who might not be able to read and write could still possess a very complex vocabulary that deals with the specific profession of the person. In most cases, such vocabularies are restricted to a small group and are primarily used in closed groups because that is where such language is most needed. In fact, if the words are used in a more general setting, the words could become completely meaningless or be totally misinterpreted.

Jargon is made of complex and specialized words that are deliberately used with a general audience. People who use jargon most often use very specialized words when speaking in a group where most of the audience would not understand what is being said. This is a phenomenon that has little to do with technology and tools. Specialized words exist in many professions, from sports to science, and those words are meant to be used among those who are expected to understand the meaning of the words. Using the same words in a different setting would make the same words sound like jargon. Yet, this is a process that goes on constantly. In many cases it is a matter of habit where a person could be so embedded in a specialized profession that the individual could simply be unaware of the time when a particular word should not be used. However, jargon is also used as a tool for alienation where people would deliberately use jargon to demonstrate to the audience that the listener is indeed alienated and thus in need of help. This strategy of using special words with special meanings is evident in all the advertisements cited earlier. There are specialized technical words interspersed in each of the three promotional materials and the language could easily further alienate a person who is already dealing with a malfunctioning piece of technology. Those who are able to use the jargon and sprinkle their talk with the special words immediately begin to wield a certain amount of power over people who are not only alienated from the technology but also do not even possess the appropriate language to describe what is wrong. The strength of jargon as a tool of power is acknowledged by the consultant to Fortune 500 Companies, Scott Berkun, who said in the *Harvard Business Blog*, "To use these words with a straight face is to assume the listener is an idiot. They are intellectual insults."[24] This is exactly how jargon works to alienate people, because it reinforces the sense of helplessness since the listener might simply not understand what a term means and automatically gives over power to someone who seems to be using the term in a confident way.

The process of alienation is not only a product of the way in which people relate to technology and tools that surround them but is also determined by the way in which people relate to each other. The different levels of alienation discussed here are akin to any other levels of marginalization where some a priori construct, such as skin color or religion, becomes conventionally stronger than the others creating a system of oppression and marginalization. Sometimes these agents of difference are supported by the instruments of raw power, as in the case of the whites of South Africa in the time of apartheid when they controlled the internal militia and were able to subjugate the non-whites. In other cases, power is given over to some through sheer apathy making groups such as the Nazis in Fascist Germany, wield power because numerous Germans had chosen to look the other way when the Nazis began the persecution of Jews. In all such cases, there is a difference in power between people with different attributes. In most cases, the power is related to immutable attributes—a dark skinned person always will remain dark skinned—and that attribute is related to the ways in which genes have evolved over the ages. The situation with alienation from technology is unique because the person alienated from technology, and thus powerless, always has the potential to overcome that alienation. Yet, because alienation creates a societal power differential, those who are not alienated have a vested interest in keeping large sections of people alienated. As indicated here, there are numerous ways that can be used to wield and retain the power that is obtained by keeping others alienated. Eventually, it becomes the onus of the alienated to overcome their distancing from technology and regain the power that is lost through alienation. The next chapter concludes with a brief and preliminary discussion of the ways in which the issue of alienation can be tackled both at the personal and at the societal level.

8

What Do I Need to Do?

A question that becomes immediately important after under-standing the issues surrounding the idea of alienation is, "Do all of us suddenly have to go to the Massachusetts Institute of Technology or the Indian Institute of Technology to be able to overcome our alienations and become users of the toaster at home?" The increasing sophistication of the tools around us can make us feel rather inadequate, especially when it would appear that there are some people who seem to be able to use the tools so much more confidently than us. There is a certain 'smugness' about those who seem to be more comfortable with the tools and are willing to flaunt that ability, making others feel nervous about their ineptness with the tools.

The sense of inadequacy that is connected with the inability to use some tools can become conflated with the idea of intelligence. There has been a significant amount of energy spent trying to understand the concept of intelligence. Socio-logists, educators, psychologists, and neuroscientists have all tried to understand what makes a person intelligent and how one must measure intelligence. There are differing definitions of the term and there is little agreement about what the source of intelligence might be. One of the common strains in the definitions is a focus on the ability to learn new things by applying a reasonable approach based in logic. This led to the attention paid to measuring a concept called "Intelligence Quotient (IQ)," and as discussed earlier, it was quickly discovered that IQ actually measures nothing and much of the IQ tests were basically the equivalent of bar games to amuse each other and mildly show off that one could quickly do calculations in one's head. Critics of these tests have been very vocal about the way in which the tests do not measure the complete range of abilities of a person. Indeed in the United States these tests, originally developed in France in the early 1900s, have taken on a central role for college admission for students coming out of high schools. However, with mounting criticism of these tests, there are some colleges, including the one where I teach, that are starting to abandon the well-known Scholastic Aptitude Test (SAT) as a deciding criteria for admitting students. Many universities are arguing that tests like the SAT offer little evidence of the true abilities of a person. Other measures were used to measure the worth of a person to decide whether one should get into college or not, or be employed or not. These are measures that attempt to enumerate the overall worth of a person as in the case of the use of the tests that try to measure the concept of Emotional Quotient (EQ) which is geared to calibrate the emotional qualities of a person. In the case of the IQ tests, there is such a strong dependence on these tests among some employers and colleges that it has led to dubious claims that one could actually become intelligent and some made a large profits selling books that would promise noticeable gains in IQ after regular practice and improving one's brain, much like one might improve the size of the biceps with the use of the correct weight training. In the case of IQ and EQ levels there is an underlying assumption that these are inherent qualities of a person, and the training can make a person a little better but if a person is born intelligent then there is no need for further training. On the other hand there is also the assumption that if a person is inherently less intelligent then the training could help somewhat, but would never be able to overcome the "genetic" handicap of being less intelligent than others. This assumption has been proven to be fallacious, but it still permeates the popular imagination about intelligence leading to a certain degree of despair in those who have always been told that they are not intelligent. Such fatalistic socialization starts early when children could be reminded by teachers that a child is not intelligent, dooming the person to a life of mediocrity. Although modern education systems are less prone to making such sweeping judgements, there is a complete social structure in place that implicitly places people in blocs where some are labeled as more intelligent than others. In some cases, where literacy rates are lower, intelligence and literacy are sometimes collapsed into a single category. This becomes particularly dangerous because someone who has not had the opportunity to gain literacy could well be a person who possesses some of the accepted defining characteristics associated with an intelligent person.

For all these reasons, I argue that the issue of alienation is different from intelligence. The key distinguishing factor is the fact that it is possible for a person to gain a fairly good measure of the level of alienation. As I have suggested in this book, the indicators of alienation hover around a set of questions that can be empirically answered by someone trying to assess the level of alienation. As a matter of fact, it is possible for any person to consider the set of questions like, "Do I know what this does?" and "Do I know how to fix this?" and be able to come up with a reasonably accurate gauge of the level of alienation. These are not questions that require a great deal of introspection as in the case of the EQ and IQ tests; the questions that can shed some light on the level of alienation are principally behavioral measures. An individual must answer the questions truthfully about the specific technology that the person is using and be able to obtain a fairly accurate sense of the level of alienation with respect to the particular tool.

The level of alienation is also not a universal construct that attempts to label the whole person as in the case of the IQ and EQ tests. These tests offer a final numeric value that becomes the indicator of the worth of the person. This number is also considered to be relatively permanent and those who measure at a lower IQ level are condemned to stay at the lower level, with perhaps minor changes that might come with great deal of practice with taking IQ tests. The notion of alienation is not related to the whole person or any innate characteristic of the person, but is actually a notion that refers to the relationship that the person has with a specific tool. Consider for instance a situation where one person could be very alienated with some tools but perfectly comfortable with others. Thus a person who might know all about repairing a car might be completely alienated from a laptop computer. Such examples suggest that alienation is related to specific tools and is not an exhaustive measurement of the technological acumen of a person. Human beings are tool-using creatures and it would be impossible to live in the contemporary world without overcoming alienation with some tools which have become ubiquitous. Thus, people can overcome alienation when the tools become essential to everyday life. This ability to overcome alienation makes it a very different construct from that of intelligence. A dangerous fallacy would be to assume that the alienated person is not an intelligent person. Indeed, the two notions remain relatively unconnected.

There are many who would not know they are alienated because they have not thought about the issue, and have not paid much attention to the tools that surround them. The demands of everyday life overtake the curiosity that leads to some of the key questions related to alienation. The customary way of doing things often becomes habitual and within the constraints of habit most people are satisfied with the way things are. It is only when something goes wrong that one becomes aware of one's habits, and the vulnerability related to alienation becomes abruptly evident. It is only when the tool fails that one notices the tool, and one has to confront one's alienation. This becomes a reactive way of life where it appears that one runs from one crisis to another without ever feeling that one is in control of one's life. Even though the sense of control is somewhat misleading, there is some value in adopting a proactive posture with relation to the way in which tools work, so that one is not completely taken unawares when things do go wrong. Overcoming alienation actually can allow a user to better understand what can potentially go wrong with a tool and be prepared to deal with that eventuality when that would happen. In many hilly areas in the United States, there are parts of the road where a car or a truck would be driving down a steep incline relying on the brakes to slow down the vehicle. Often there would be a rest area after such a stretch of the road and in most cases there is a sign that reminds drivers to check their brakes before entering the rest area. What this warning suggests is the understanding that brakes could have become frayed after use on the road, and it is best to check them before entering a congested area where a failure of the brake could lead to disastrous results. Not all drivers might be thinking about this consequence but the warning sign makes them mindful of the consequences of the failure of the car brake which many drivers take for granted. This mindfulness is an important step towards the process of recognizing and overcoming one's alienation. This attitude towards technology can also allow one to actually use the tool in a more satisfying manner by overcoming the preliminary sets of alienation and becoming more accustomed to the technological system when one is using it.

Another significant difference between the accepted notion of intelligence and alienation is the fact that intelligence is always considered to be internal to a person and one who would be considered unintelligent might carry that stigma in all aspects of life. If a child does not perform well in mathematics then the child is called un-smart in certain academic cultures. That child almost automatically gets stigmatized and superior performance in other areas of study and interest might not even register as important and noteworthy because the child has been labeled as unintelligent. There is something inherently incorrect and unfair about such judgements because it becomes an internalized characteristic of the person. There is also an assumption that such a person is doomed to live an unintelligent life and it is nearly impossible to overcome the lack of intelligence. Alienation, however, works in a different way and it is possible to overcome alienation in different stages. As pointed out in this book, alienation is relative to an external technological system. It is possible to overcome the sense of alienation by becoming literate of the technology or by moving on to technologies from which an individual is less alienated. This is not a condition that should be considered beyond correction. There are many reasons why a person might feel alienated from different technological systems. And a person might feel alienated at different levels, but it is possible to overcome this condition. Graduating out of alienation begins with a clear recognition of the issue and the realization that the issue is personalized, but is often a collective phenomenon resulting from a multitude of reasons. Overcoming alienation begins with realizing that one is indeed alienated.

MAGICAL TOOLS

The process of confronting one's alienation begins by realizing that tools and technological systems are not magical processes that have to remain mysterious. There is an aura to technology that often takes on a mystical quality where the alienated would truly believe that some of the things that tools do appear to be so fantastic that they are magical. Much of the awe comes from lack of familiarity with the tools. Consider for instance a way in which certain infections are treated. Many people would suffer from an infection that defies all treatment. In a 2009 article that appeared in the *Popular Science* magazine there was a story about a specific kind of virus called phages.[25] These viruses have the unique quality of feeding on specific kinds of bacteria. Much of infections are caused by bacteria which would infest a wound and stubbornly resist all antibacterial medicines. For some patients this could mean a slow and painful degradation of the quality of life and even fatality. A doctor in the United States was dealing with such a patient with a chronic leg wound. No traditional treatment with antibacterial medicines would repair the wound. Eventually, the American doctor consulted with doctors in Eastern Europe where scientists are researching the use of phages to treat specific bacterial infection. A specific combination of phages was developed after identifying the offending bacteria and the phage solution was applied to the wound. Within days of applying the phage treatment the patient recovered from what was being considered to be an untreatable wound. The magazine describes the outcome as "astonishing," and to the alienated it would almost appear as magical as applying an elixir to a wound and bringing to life a dead person. It is such technological moments that generate a sense of magic. Yet, just like the phage treatment, most technological systems follow certain fundamental logical processes that most people are capable of understanding if one is willing to take a little bit of time to examine the system and learn more about the system. Much of technological systems rely on fundamental scientific principles that have been developed into tools for everyday use. The scientists that have developed the system might have been people who were driven by the desire to invent something new, but once the invention results in products and services that become ubiquitous, the user needs to understand the origin of the process and realize that what appears to be magical is indeed driven by very well-defined scientific principles. For example, the cell phone works on the basis of fundamental principles of physics and no magic can make the cell phone do anything more than what the scientific principles allow. This realization is not the same as understanding the principles in great detail, but only realizing that there are principles that govern the systems. Alienation is often the result of forgetting that there are verifiable principles that allow the tools to do what they do, and the person who is willing to overcome alienation usually first takes on a scientific attitude that acknowledges that there are rational principles that determine how tools work.

The willingness to overcome the alienation could result in acquiring information about specific tools that surround us. A little familiarity with the tools immediately demonstrates to most people that there is nothing magical about the tools, and they all work on the basis of a set of rules that determine the way in which the system functions. Overcoming alienation is essentially understanding the logic of a technological system and sometimes this understanding could make life much simpler. Some of the logic is scientific logic that restricts what a tool can or cannot do. For example, there is still no reliable scientific theory that would help to produce a system that could travel faster than the speed of light. Thus, the fantastic rockets of movies like *Star Wars* are indeed magical because they defy the laws of physics and remain within the confines of the imagination of the science fiction writer. There are other logical systems that also motivate the way in which certain technological systems work. These are logics that can predict normal human behavior where social scientists have been able to provide sufficient evidence that people would behave in certain ways when given the appropriate prompts. Once there is sufficient support that there is some degree of predictability in human behavior drawn from the research in communication, sociology, and psychology, it is possible to construct technological systems that follow these principles. Consider for example the system I described earlier that has become universally popular for customer service providers—automated telephone systems. Typically, in these systems a person needing customer service would call a phone number to get help and be greeted with a recorded message that asks the caller to punch in a series of numbers like the caller's phone number, national identity number and other such information. The basic sociological system that structures these systems is the knowledge that people usually follow instructions. Most people would follow the voice prompts that are offered by the automated system and these rely on this logic to reduce the need for customer service workers, whose work can be done by computers that can respond to the caller based on the way in which a compliant customer responds to the prompts. These systems rarely offer the opportunity to speak to a human being and all the work is handled by computer systems that respond to the keys pressed by the user. One could ask how the system works, and one would find out that pressing a button on the telephone sends a specific signal to a computer system initiating a series of events that help to channel the caller through different likely scenarios. On the other hand, if the computer does not get the input from the user, then the computer would eventually channel the call to a real person. There is both a scientific logic based on the principles of computer engineering and a sociological logic that makes these systems appear magical. Once an individual is aware that this is indeed a logical system it is possible to use the system in a different way. Thus, the easiest way to get to a human being, in most cases, is not to press any keys, but hold on until a human being answers the phone. The lack of the expected response defies the internal logic of the system and the user who is not alienated from the logic can use the knowledge to make the system do what the user wants, rather than being held hostage by what might appear to be a magical system. Understanding the process, without necessarily having to know the exact computer system that makes this work, is sufficient to demystify the technology and make it more accessible and reduce the sense of alienation.

Those who are able to overcome the sense of alienation are essentially people who have harnessed their understanding of the technological world by exploring the basic foundations of the tool. It is not so much that they have suddenly become technologists, but they have taken the effort to realize that most of the tools that surround us are indeed no more than mere tools—made by us to serve us—as opposed to magical machines that seem to do things automatically. The most telling example of the myth of magical power of machines is obtained when thinking about computers. The alienated often are amazed by what the computer can do, from showing videos on the screen to storing huge amounts of information, appearing almost "intelligent." What is missed in such "mythologization" of computers is the fact that the computer does exactly what it is instructed to do by the user and the programmers who put together the commands that the computer must follow. The computer is not a creative tool; it is the human user who creates with the computer. This simple separation between the creative user and the dumb computer is often neglected, or obfuscated, in the minds of the alienated who transfer power to the computer, and eventually to those people who have overcome alienation and have seen through the logical system that drives computers. Overcoming alienation is not only successfully answering the questions related to each stage of alienation as discussed in this book but also actually gaining agency over technology where the magical work is done by the people who use the tools, and the tools remain lifeless machines whose function and use is determined by the user and not vice versa. It is this leap, from being controlled by technology to controlling technology that accompanies overcoming the alienation from the technological systems we have to live with.

CRITICAL USER

It is also this leap that allows the un-alienated to become a critical user of tools as opposed to those who use the tools simply because they exist. There is a constant innovation of tools that are thrust before users who are promised that their quality of life would be immensely improved if they begin to use the new tools. Massive corporations are constantly tweaking the tools that they make and the companies continue to offer slightly improved versions of their tools hoping to entice the consumer in buying the products. In some cases, completely new tools are developed that offer to do new things and people are promised that the new tool would certainly make life easier. As pointed out earlier, the alienated user is often enticed by such promises and becomes subject to the corporations that constantly inundate the consumer with the messages of the "promise of technology." Overcoming the alienation allows the user to be able to better understand these messages and consider if the new technology is indeed needed. A significant outcome of overcoming alienation is becoming the critical consumer who is able to make an informed judgement about the role of a new technology in one's life, because new tools necessarily change the way we live.

Tools invariably alter the practices of everyday life. Electricity has fundamentally changed the way in which people live and that change is most evident when electricity is unavailable. There are numerous other technological systems from household plumbing to the iPhone that has altered the way we live. The alienated users of tools often end up making changes in their lives only because the tools exist, and their lives become shaped by the tools where everyday activities are blindly entwined with the use of the tools. These are the people who would be helpless when a tool ceases to work because doing certain tasks become impossible without the tool. Consider the situation with a person who has misplaced a cell phone. This is a condition that can render a person completely helpless because the cell phone had records of all the phone numbers that the person might need. Over time, a cell phone becomes a phone book and the phone numbers recorded on the phone might not exist anywhere else at all. The loss of a cell phone becomes traumatic not because the phone instrument is misplaced but because all the numbers are lost. It is not too difficult to replace the phone by buying a new phone, but it might be impossible to restore all the lost numbers. Yet, there are simple ways to keep those numbers backed up on a computer or even on the Internet to prepare for the eventuality of the lost phone. However, one needs to overcome some of the levels of alienation in order to recognize the role of the cell phone in one's life and to ensure that periodic back-ups are done to maintain a record of the numbers stored in the phone. The un-alienated user is much more mindful of the "phone book" function of the cell phone and does the things needed to make sure the cell phone is appropriately used. Overcoming alienation allows the user to better understand how the technology adds value to everyday life, and if indeed the technology is needed.

The issue of 'needing' a tool is especially important to consider when a new tool is brought before the user. As discussed in this book the question of newness is intertwined with the level of alienation of the user. Many tools appear new simply because of alienation and the user is unable to clearly distinguish between the old and the new because both appear equally magical and the new one appears to do more of the magic of technology. There is little critical consideration of the tool by the alienated because the individual simply does not have sufficient information to make the determination. This is the ideal customer for new technologies. Salespeople are thrilled by the alienated consumer who could be sold any new technology simply by convincing the person that the tool is new, and without ever having to go into any detail about what exactly is 'new' about the tool. Consider, for example, an advertisement for a hybrid car made by BMW and promoted in a British newspaper that claims that the car is 'lot more fun' than its competition. Those three words provide scant information about what exactly sets the car aside from its competition in a technical sense. Yet, there is no special need on the part of the advertiser to worry too much about explaining the technical details because there is an assumption that most readers of the newspaper are indeed alienated from the technology and the best way to reach them is indeed to avoid the technical talk as in the case of the advertisement of the Tata Motors Xenon brand of vehicles which calls its "all new" car, "a kindred spirit." This language purposefully avoids any special language simply because alienation from technology has become an accepted and expected condition for most people. To such a population anything can be sold as "new and improved" making it a fantastic arena for promoting new tools to a relatively hapless market.

Clearly something needs to change about the condition that many face when confronted with tools. It is far too common to hear people laugh off their alienation and pretend that it does not matter. The reality is, however, that it *does* matter and it is important to recognize the fact—remaining alienated is remaining powerless. A father who does not know how to use text messaging on a cell phone, a mother who has never gone on to a social networking website or a shopper who unwittingly gives up personal information for a free trinket are always at a disadvantage in a world that is becoming rapidly dependant on numerous tools. The first step in the process of reclaiming the power is to diagnose the condition, and ask the question, "What is a person's level of alienation?" There is no doubt, based on the law of technological alienation, that everyone is somewhat alienated, but it is important to recognize that condition before finding a treatment for the condition. The dilemma is that the loss of power that happens with alienation is an incremental loss and does not happen all at once. If one gets robbed at gunpoint, it is a violent moment where one starkly realizes that the individual was rendered powerless. The loss of power because of alienation happens much more slowly but keeps building up until one is completely bewildered by what has happened around them and there is a virtual "technological death" from which it is impossible to recover. This is somewhat analogous to a disease such as high blood pressure or elevated cholesterol in the blood—conditions that can kill slowly unless detected and treated on time. Thus the first question to ask is, "How alienated am I?" Knowing that can help to set one on the path of recovery where technology loses its mystery and the individual can control the technology as opposed to the alien technology consuming one's life.

HOW ALIENATED AM I?

One of the best ways of trying to gauge this is to go through a process of introspection where a person would actually start with taking an inventory of the tools that surround the person. This list would vary widely primarily based on demographic attributes. Growing up in India in the 1960s and 1970s the question was easily answered in a developing nation where a middle-class urban home would have a limited set of tools. The same period in America saw a technological boom where average homes would be acquiring numerous tools that promised to add to the quality of life. Homes in the West would have tools such as automatic dish washers, washing machines, vacuum cleaners, and other household appliances that would make everyday life easier but would also add to the sense of alienation. This same boom arrived in other countries in the 1980s and 1990s as more people were able to afford more tools. The combination of availability of the tools and increasing affluence led to a condition where more people were able to acquire a greater number of tools for personal use. A good example of this process is seen in the case of the telephone. In the United States, there were always a large number of public telephone booths available to people to make phone calls. These would be available at almost every street corner in most cities, and those who needed to make a quick phone call would be able to use these phones, paying for the phone call using coins. That started to change with the greater penetration of cell phones when most people had their personal phones that they would carry with them. The need for the public phone booth diminished to the point where phone companies began to dismantle these booths because they became completely unprofitable. This process demonstrates how one public technology, which many people had become familiar with, has been replaced by a private technology from which many are still alienated. In this manner, people have been increasingly inundated with private tools that have become commonplace. Digital music players show up in the pockets and purses of teenagers all over the world. The process of understanding the level of alienation begins with taking stock of what we have surrounded ourselves with. Most people do not consciously think about the number of technological systems that one has to constantly use and rely on to live a normal life. Independent of which country one lives in, most of the urban population across the globe relies on electricity that is fundamental to current civilizations; people have to rely on methods of cleaning drinking water and methods of keeping the urban areas clean. Those people who have paid more attention to the ways in which technological systems can become harmful are also the ones who are less alienated from the technological systems and can actually use the tools in a wise way. This wisdom about technology begins with carefully considering the tools we use and the consequences of using the tools.

Next it is important to ask how much we know of the tools. Each stage of alienation deals with a fundamental question and those questions must be asked about all the tools that are around us. This is a complex process because the numbers of tools have gone up dramatically, and it is quite likely that the answers could be quite different for the different tools. Consider for instance a basic tool such as a hammer. There is not much mystery to a hammer from which most people would not be alienated. It is an instrument that can be used to drive a nail into wood. Even a child would be able to work that out if given a little bit of time. People usually know all there is to know about the hammer, and it takes little time to understand that the harder one hits, the quicker can one drive in a nail and it is important to hit the nail in the correct way to make sure it goes in straight. The way the hammer works is relatively simple to decipher. The matter becomes different when one considers a nail gun. This is an instrument that does the same thing as the hammer. This is an electrical tool that looks like a gun, but instead of shooting bullets it shoots nails and can be used to rapidly drive nails into wood. It is much more efficient in performing the same function as the hammer, but it does the function in a completely different way. Although the function of the hammer and the nail is identical, it is often the case that the user would know much less about the nail gun than about the hammer. At such moments it is useful to recognize that even though tools might have the same function, they might complete the function in such dramatically different ways that it is important to ask the questions related to each stage of alienation about the different tools around us and recognize that there are variable answers to the questions even though the tools appear to do the same thing. This variability needs to be confronted and we need to realize that there are many tools from which we are completely alienated. For example, a user might have overcome alienation from a traditional camera and had learnt how to put the film in the camera and take pictures, but could be completely alienated from the way in which pictures are taken by a digital camera. We have adopted those tools because we have been convinced that we must have those tools. Our lives have become so complicated that it is impossible to live without the tools and we must now overcome our alienation. As a starting point, it is useful to consider the Alienation Inventory at the end of the book to get an alienation scale for oneself.

A careful introspection of the level of alienation can eventually become somewhat depressing. It does not take too long to realize that one is alienated from most of the tools that have become commonplace. At that moment it is easy to say that it is a hopeless condition that one can never overcome. However, there are some simple ways to begin to overcome the alienation as suggested in Chapter 9.

9

Preliminary Steps

*T*he most important step towards overcoming the sense of alienation is recognizing the fact that alienation can indeed be overcome. This is a simple component of self-esteem and belief in the fact that there is nothing individualized about being unfamiliar with the tools that surround us. A combination of curiosity and looking around for information can help to reduce the level of alienation that accompanies the encounter with new gadgets and technological systems. The evidence for this claim is often seen among younger people when they are confronted with new technologies. Very often young people are able to adopt the use of new tools not because they are necessarily smarter than others, but because they do not have the innate fear and resistance that older people have towards change. In many cases, alienation is indeed a matter of resisting change, and the sense of alienation can well become a crutch that people rely on in order to avoid having to adapt to new technological systems. Claiming that one does not understand the system is a particularly good way of avoiding using a system. This is an internalized tendency that has little to do with a specific technology or gadget, but has much more to do with the way in which a person deals with change. Yet, there is sufficient evidence to show that those who are willing to overcome the sense of alienation are able to do so. Unfortunately, there is no systematic way of overcoming alienation. It is not yet the case that one can go to a special school, or take a particular course that would magically allow a person to overcome their alienation from specific tools. It is relatively difficult to conceive of such systems since the technologies change rapidly and the process of overcoming alienation needs to be thought of in a holistic way as opposed to looking at alienation with respect to specific tools. Even if one overcomes the alienation with respect to a single tool, it is quite likely that the individual would get alienated when a new tool comes along. Thus, it is better to consider some general approaches towards relationship between tools and people to provide means of getting over the sense of alienation from many different technological systems.

THE LANGUAGE OF TECHNOLOGY

Thinkers such as Michel Foucault have suggested that there is a close connection between language and power. According to Foucault, those who are able to control language and the discourse it produces in a social system are often able to wield power over others who are subjectified by the language. As pointed out earlier, much of the process of alienation has to deal with the way in which language is used to talk about technology and how language can become the tool of alienation. The most important step towards overcoming alienation is understanding the way in which language is used to discuss issues of technology.

There are generally two kinds of language use and both have specific power connotations. On one hand the discourse on technology could be conducted in a manner that is particularly complex and impenetrable. This is not even the issue of jargon that was discussed earlier, but the creation of a specific vocabulary that is reserved for the inner circle of technologists who use the language because that represents the vocabulary of their specialty. For example, engineers working on a specific building project must use some special language to communicate with each other to make the communication efficient. The non-technologist need not be a part of that conversation, but often there are ways in which that language would bleed into interactions where specialists would slip into their unique language in the presence of those who are unfamiliar with the special dialect. This happens often in the case of medical technology. Often, physicians would enter into a discussion of a treatment in the presence of the patient or the family where those listening to the discussion would be immediately alienated and rendered powerless because the language of the physicians remains meaningless but sounds superior. This is a tendency where the alienation is produced simply because the specialists are either willingly or involuntarily creating a situation where alienation is a natural outcome.

A completely different way in which language produces alienation is when the discourse is reduced to terms that become banal and meaningless in actually discussing a tool or a technological system. I have discussed this condition earlier in talking about advertisements where the language of the promotional material is so simple that the real purpose of the technology, or some of its basic components are hidden from sight. In such cases, the user of the technology is rendered powerless by oversimplification of the discourse resulting in hiding significant components of the new technology from the potential user. This is the kind of language that encourages the user of the tool to assume that there is something mystical about technology and the use of the particular tool will change the life of the users, even though the user might not necessarily know how the change is occurring.

It is relatively difficult to encounter discourse that appears to actually speak to the user of a tool in a way that explains the interaction between the tool and the user. This would be a situation where everyday language is skillfully used to convey the relevant information to the user of the tool so that the user has a clear sense of all the different aspects of the tool from its function to the best ways of getting it mended. There is a woeful lack of such discourse because there has really not been much of a demand for it, and historically users have been placed in the powerless position which many have just acquiesced to.

The first move towards overcoming the process of alienation thus does not even start with making changes to one's personal knowledge of technology, but with demanding a better way of talking about technology. This is not an internal change within users, but an external change within the technological infrastructure which could become more sensitive to the users' demands when the users express sufficient amount of frustration with the way in which they are being systematically left out from a clearer understanding of a specific technological system. It is not necessarily the case that the users are unable to understand the appropriate discourse about technology, but they simply have not been offered the opportunity to understand it. Overcoming alienation begins with the demand for greater transparency with respect to technological systems that surround us. The users need to demand that those who control and promote technological systems find the appropriate mix of language so that users can better comprehend the relationship between the individual and the tool.

This move has to come from a collection of technology users who recognize that they are alienated not because of their own shortcomings but because they are embedded in a system where discourse has been hijacked by those who are willing to confuse and make things more complicated than they have to be. There is some evidence of this frustration as groups are formally resisting the hold that specialists wield on language.

Consider, for example, a move made by the Local Government Association (LGA) in Britain. The LGA is responsible for setting the policy for Councils that are responsible for local governance in Britain. In a declaration made in 2009, the LGA instructed the Councils to stop using 200 different words that are considered to be unnecessarily alienating for the population. In their directive, the LGA suggested words like "menu of options," and "systematics." These are examples of words that the LGA deemed to be particularly unclear, which offer the speaker a position of undue power based simply on the fact that most users would not know what these words actually refer to. Quite naturally there has been some resistance to this move and members of the Information Technology (IT) industry have been troubled by the ban. Reporting on this matter, Tim Collins of the Web-based magazine, *Computerweekly.com*, indicated that representatives of the IT industry have claimed that many of the words included in the ban are essential to describe the different technological systems that are used by the industry.[26] There is thus a tension that needs to be resolved in the way in which the technology industry and the user interact with each other as the question of language and alienation is examined more carefully. Outright banning might not be as productive as developing a more nuanced approach to dealing with the way in which language automatically creates alienations. Such approaches would require the cooperation of both the technology industry and the users where the groups can enter into a dialog to examine the ways in which the two groups can work with each other for the benefit of both.

There is some evidence of that process developing too as more people are recognizing the consequences of alienation based on a language barrier. A global cell phone company recognized that nearly half their customers were unfamiliar with the full range of functions of their phone instrument, and were alienated from the tool making them inefficient users of the cell phones. Consequently the company made a specific move to train their staff in using simple language to help the users get the most out of their gadgets. Initiatives like that point towards an effort on the part of the technology infrastructure to help reduce the alienation of the potential users of the technology. Such moves also allow the user to be better able to develop the appropriate questions to ask about the technological system. Often, through demanding answers to critical questions it is possible to reduce alienation.

QUESTIONS TO ASK

One of the most important questions about a tool or technological system is to find out all the functions performed by the tool or system. This is a particularly pragmatic question where a user should know what a tool does. As pointed out throughout the book, it is increasingly difficult to find a clear answer to this question because of a variety of reasons, ranging from the increasing complexity of the tool to the lack of clear communication about the tool and functionality. In some cases, it is difficult to get a complete answer to this question because some functionality might be so specialized that even the experts might not be clear on the specific functions. The user must, however, insist on finding a satisfactory answer to the question, "What does this do?"

This is also a question that an individual cannot be expected to answer without external help. It is impossible for most users of sophisticated tools to know all the functions of the tool. This needs to be clearly described by the person or the group that designed and built the tool. They are the ones who would know the different things a tool could do. It is the responsibility of the makers of the tool to clearly communicate that information to all users. Yet, this communication is often incomplete and there are numerous users who are unaware of the full potential of the systems they interact with. The challenge for the user is seeking out the information. With sophisticated tools it is increasingly difficult to find a central depository for this information.

The obvious starting point for answering the question about functionality is to start with the guidebook that accompanies most tools and technological systems. The purpose of the guidebook is to let the user know what the tool can do and how to use the tool. There have, however, been changes made to guidebooks that actually encourage alienation where these books have been made shorter and simpler to a point where the books only talk about the most commonly used functions of the system and leave it to the user to discover the more complex, and often the more useful, functions of the system. Consider the case of the DVD player. Most DVDs in the late 1990s were manufactured in a way that DVDs made in Asia would only work on DVD players made in Asia. This process is called "region coding," making it impossible for a person to purchase a Bollywood movie on DVD in Delhi and hope to play it on a DVD player purchased in New York. There was a sufficient amount of frustration about this restriction that some users were trying to find a way around it. A rumor started at this same time that a Chinese manufacturer was actually selling a DVD player in American stores that had the capability of overriding the region restriction. Interestingly, the manual that accompanied the DVD player had no mention of this special functionality of the tool. Indeed this specific capability of the tool was hidden away in a "secret menu" which had to be accessed through a careful sequence of key presses on the remote control to be greeted with a statement on the screen that said, "YOU SHOULD NOT BE HERE." The user would then be able to override the region restriction of the DVD player and happily watch DVDs from anywhere in the world. There was absolutely no way for the user to learn of this capability of the DVD player by reading the user's guide or by simply tinkering with the machine. The user could only get this information by browsing for additional information at websites that discussed the DVD player.

The sophistication of the tools and the existence of such "hidden" functionalities can often only be found when the user actively seeks out this information. While it is the responsibility of the maker of the system to provide the complete information, it is also the case that the manufacturer cannot be relied upon to provide this information. A user who wants to truly overcome the sense of alienation has to take on the task of demystifying the functions of the tool. The user can ask the expert to offer the answer to the questions but sometimes the experts are unwilling to answer all the questions because the answer could go against the self-interest of those who make the tools. Consider the case of the cell phone. In 2009, the official statistics showed that nearly 6 out of 10 people in the world owned a cell phone. A large portion of these phones have the capability of establishing a high-speed connection to the Internet using the built-in wireless Internet connection system called Wi-Fi. Once the cell phone is connected via Wi-Fi the phone can perform like a mini-computer and allow the owner to use services that allow phone calls over the Internet at a cost much lower than the cost of making a call using the service provided by the seller of the cell phone. In other words, the computer-like capability of the cell phone allows the user to use the cell phone instrument to bypass the costlier service provided by the cell phone seller. It is naturally not in the interest of the cell phone seller like T-Mobile or Airtel to flaunt this capability of the handset that they are selling. Thus the user cannot rely on the seller or the manufacturer to disclose the complete information about the capabilities of a new tool.

Attempting to overcome alienation by seeking information about functionality thus becomes something that the user has to take on as a specific task that would help to reduce alienation. This is an active process where the user needs to be able to seek out a different set of information sources and find out more about a tool that the user already owns or might be considering acquiring. In the case of the latter condition, the question of functionality needs to be supplemented with a larger question about the role of a specific tool in the everyday life of the user. It is important to always remember that a tool is supposed to simplify some activity for the user. The tool should have a positive effect on the quality of life of the user. This user needs to consider this matter carefully and think of the ways in which the tool will add to the quality of life. Answering this question helps to overcome the sense of alienation related to not knowing what to do with many of the functionalities of the tool. Again, the cell phone provides a good example. Most cell phones sold since 2007 have a camera built into them. This camera can not only take mediocre to nice digital pictures, but the user can also immediately send the picture to another cell phone as a part of a multimedia message (MMS). There is, however, increasing evidence that a small percentage of cell phone owners actually do this task. People might be using the cell phone to take pictures, but not many are sending them on as a part of an MMS message. Yet this capability distinguishes the cell phone from a standard digital camera which would typically not be able to transmit the picture. The user needs to consider how the added functionality (and cost, since each MMS has to be paid for) would add to the quality of life. This is a process where each functionality is ascribed a 'quality of life' attribute to see if the function would indeed have a positive effect on the quality of life, or make things so complicated that it would detract from the quality of life.

The process of doing the homework to seek out information about a tool or technological system is the first step towards reducing alienation. The next phase is asking questions about the tool to see how the tool works—not so much with respect to the technology, but with respect to the fundamental logic that determines the operation of the tool or the system.

Inquiring about the function of a tool or a technological system needs to be accompanied with finding out more about the way in which the tool provides the functions. This is the "how" question that relates to the essential logic of a system and how the logical work is performed. For most people this also becomes the most challenging aspect because there is a sense that some are not technologically adept at understanding the "how" component of a tool and are thus destined to always be alienated. As pointed out earlier, this is often a learned disability and is promoted more by a societal system rather than based on an intrinsic disability to understand the way in which a tool works.

Users need to probe the basic principles that make a tool do what it is supposed to do. These are usually scientific principles that translate to practical things that need to be done to a tool to make it work in the way intended. The many examples used in this book point towards the ways in which the users are often unwilling to ask the question about the way in which a tool works, and thus find themselves in positions where they unwittingly appear alienated simply because they have never thought of asking the question about the way in which the tool does what it is supposed to do.

On the first level, the user must inquire about the different pieces that make up a gadget. Often this information is provided in a user's manual which would have a picture showing the different components of a tool. In the case of electronic gadgets these diagrams often point towards the numerous buttons and displays that might be built into the tool and the user should be able to identify what all the buttons do. It is usually not sufficient to know what only the important buttons do, but also be sure about the other buttons that one might not use often but which could be required to use in special situations and under conditions when there might not be enough time to figure out which button would provide the function. A good example of this is also obtained from the ubiquitous cell phone. Consider for instance the numerous times one would see a user fumbling with a cell phone that starts ringing and disturbs an ongoing meeting. It is not unusual to see an embarrassed user leave the room because the person is unable to determine the way to shut off the offending ringing sound. That shows a level of alienation that could easily be corrected if the user pays a little attention to the different ways of using a tool and to understanding that the tool is made up of parts that do their specific tasks. Even if one were not able to find the correct button to shut off the ringer, it could be possible to place a finger tightly on the speaker of the phone and significantly reduce the volume of the ringing sound.

The user should also inquire about the parts of any tool to know how the different components are connected together. Most mechanical tools like cars are made up of numerous pieces and these are all connected together in a systematic way to make the system operate in an efficient way doing all the things that the technological system must do. It is important for the user to ask about the connection between the different systems so that the user does not inadvertently disable an important component making the entire tool inoperable or even dangerous. More people have an access to a greater number of tools and unless people are willing to ask the questions about how a tool works, it is quite possible that they will use the tool in an inappropriate way putting themselves and others at risk. This is well demonstrated in the case of use of medical tools like the antibacterial medication where people in some countries have used this so indiscriminately, without pausing to ask how the tool works, that there are now new generations of bacteria that have become resistant to the medicines that were designed to treat bacterial infection.

Part of the problem with asking the 'how' question is a degree of apprehension about understanding the answer to the question. Since the experts have colonized the language about technology, any query about technology could be met with answers that could at best be unintelligible or at worst scare off the person asking the question convincing the inquisitive person that the individual is alienated and dumb. It is the onus of the user to be able to demand a clear answer to the "how" question. It is a fair question to ask and the specialists should be able to provide a clear answer, or at least provide the user with the resources to find the answer. The most important aspect of asking this question is to be sure that the answer that is provided is indeed clear and that the user can use the information to improve the interaction with the tool, and understand the logic that drives the operations of the tool.

A part of the "how" question has to do with the specific pragmatic way in which a tool works. Another important aspect of the "how" question is to understand the underlying scientific logic that makes the tool work. This question must not be confused with a question about the details of the scientific principles but this question deals with seeking an understanding of the limitations to a tool, and remembering that the tool has nothing magical about it. Everything a tool does can be explained by principles of science which govern the functions of the inanimate object.

Tools do not have preferences about who uses the machine. There are technological ways in which it is possible to restrict the use of a particular machine to a particular person, but such means are developed by the user. The use of a password is a good example of the way in which a computer can only be used by one person. Most computers based on the Windows system require a password to access the information stored on the hard drive of the machine. This "marries" a machine to a person. Many computer users would also spend time personalizing their machine with the use of special kinds of pictures that appear on the background on the computer screen, or add little applications that help to establish a 'personal' connection between a machine and a person. This is, however, a strictly one-sided relationship! The computer operates in a logical way, and if it passes into the hands of a different user, then the new user would be able to personalize the machine in a different way. The fundamental logic that drives the computer is completely devoid of emotions and there is nothing about the machine that connects it to a person. The reason the same computer seems to work better with one person than with another is only because one person is less alienated from the computer and is able to understand its workings better than the other person. It is often the alienated person that is unable to remember that the best way to deal with a computer is to understand the reason why it does certain things, and not feel that the user is at fault. A complex relationship develops between a machine and a person because it is often the case that the alienated person would blame the machine for not working properly where indeed the reason lies with the fact that there is a systematic way in which people are alienated from the machines they have to use. One important step in overcoming alienation is to recognize that the user has to become aware of the basic logic that drives the machine and then use that knowledge to interact in an efficient way with the machine. The challenge is finding the source of the information about the machine. Often a user has to rummage through many different pieces of information before a complete picture emerges. In many cases the best way to get this information is to actually go to other users of the same machine and see what others have discovered about the tool. Since many of the issues of alienation come to the forefront when a technological system ceases to work in the expected way, a good way of learning about a tool is to talk to other users and see what problems they might have had with a tool and its functionalities.

A machine that appears to do all it is supposed to do, without creating unusual challenges for the user, does not usually lead to any curiosity about the way it works or its operational logic. It is only a tool that does not appear to be working at the expected level that generates the reason to ask questions about its functions and the way functions are performed. Often, the manufacturer of the tool is not the best place to get all the information since there are some institutional imperatives that could lead to the manufacturer being somewhat cagey about discussing all the functionalities. It is often better to ask other users of the tool about all the different things a tool could do and the problems that other users might have faced in using the tool.

It is important to understand the different kinds of users before deciding upon whom to ask. Earlier in the book, I discussed the early adopter as the user who is often willing to take the risk with a new tool to see how well it works, and how a new tool might have an impact on the everyday life of the user. The early adopters are usually curious people who are interested in taking a certain degree of risk with a tool just to discover the different functionalities of the tool. These are people who are identified by the technological industry as the ones who are most likely to be expert users of a technological innovation, and these are the people who help the industry to develop the tool to a point where an average user is able to remain alienated and yet use the tool. This strategy is most often used by the software industry that is interested in introducing a new computer program in the market. Many companies would often provide a test version of the program—often called a "beta" version—that would be made freely available to a set of early adopters who would test all the known, and some unknown, functionalities of the software. Many industries recognized the value of using beta versions of different technologies to be especially sensitive to the needs of the consumer. In an article published in the *Harvard Business Review* in 2000, Professors Prahalad and Ramaswamy made the argument that some industries are becoming increasingly sensitive to the fact that the customer is becoming competent with the use of technological products leading to the technology industry to be more aware of the customer needs.[27]

What the professors call "competence" in their article is similar to the idea of alienation. Most of the expert beta users are the un-alienated users who are able to delve deep into the functions, logic, and construction of a technological system to discover the benefits and burdens of using the tool.

The alienated user needs to turn to the early adopters to learn more about a tool before adopting it. The experience of the beta users often points towards some aspects of the tool that would not even be made clear by the maker of the tool because they might not have had the opportunity to test all aspects of the tool. This is particularly true for computers and computer programs that are constantly being developed to improve the functionalities of digital systems. Sometimes in the haste to keep up with the competition, a software developer would release a system in the marketplace without adequately testing it. The alienated user would quickly start using the tool but discover that there are flaws that can have devastating effects such as making a computer vulnerable to virus attacks. This has happened often with software released by companies like Microsoft where popular tools for opening websites have proven to have flaws that make the computer of the user easily accessible to outsiders. Sometimes, such vulnerabilities remain completely unknown to the alienated user, and are discovered by beta users who then inform the manufacturer. At that point, the manufacturer might be able to release patches that would solve the problem. As discussed earlier, all users must then use the patch to be able to protect their machines. Sometimes, the alienated user would not do that, compromising the security of many other machines. It is always a good idea for the alienated user to be able to get the information from the beta users to see what to expect with a new tool before attempting to use the tool.

One of the main questions to ask of the expert users relates to all the different functions of the tool. The alienated user is often left unaware of the many different things a tool could potentially do, and that information is not completely provided by the manufacturer either. It is the early users who are often more capable of answering the functionality questions and help other users overcome the alienation related to the different things a tool could do. This kind of information is available through different sources, many of which are available on the Internet. Anyone with Internet access can obtain detailed information about new tools and technological systems before starting to use the tool. Many technology magazines offer this information through product reviews, and the Internet has certainly made it simpler to obtain this information. Those without access to the Internet could easily make it a point to ask within their existing social networks to seek out those who are early adopters and ask them about a new tool. The key is to ask a user as opposed to an expert. The experts often regress into the same problems with jargon and language to demonstrate their expertise, thus not being particularly helpful to the alienated user. It is other experienced users, who often do not have the technological training and expertise, that turn out to be more reliable sources of information about the functions of the tool.

It is also often these people who are good at helping the alienated users with different ways of fixing a broken tool. One only has to look on the Web to find numerous sites that are maintained by users who constantly discuss different problems with specific tools and discover ways of solving the problems. These solutions are not necessarily the ones that are approved by the manufacturer of the tool, but often help to restore the functionality of the tool. An alienated user can obtain significant amount of information from these resources that is often much more usable than rummaging through the "Troubleshooting" segment of the manufacturer's guide book.

The people who are able to help the alienated user in identifying the problem and then perhaps fixing it are often those who started off being alienated as well, but took the trouble of asking questions and seeking out different answers about the tools. Eventually they overcome alienation from a particular technological system. However, these are people who not only tackle a specific tool but also gain the understanding that alienation from technology can be overcome with a little bit of effort. A person who begins to overcome alienation from technology is actually one who is able to reclaim the space that has been co-opted by technologies for themselves. The awe generated by modern technology is replaced by a sober understanding of how tools do what they are supposed to do and why tools often become difficult to work with. Overcoming alienation from technology is indeed a process of gaining a new rationalism that allows a user to look at technological developments as a part of a larger interconnected fabric of life where the tools are really meant to enhance a good quality of life rather than create problems because of our indiscriminate and blind use of tools. The user who is ready and willing to overcome alienation is the technologically literate user who is willing to constantly remain updated with the technological changes and retain power over technology rather than succumbing to it.

The power to overcome alienation and reduce the distance between a person and the surrounding technology eventually lies with a person. The technology will change as has been demonstrated in the way in which human civilization has progressed over time. This is a relatively unstoppable process and there is little reason to hold back the developments in science and technology just because people are feeling alienated. The developments have the potential of doing a lot of good for people at large as long as the tools are used properly. There is also no special reason to feel that people are unable to overcome the alienation. The works of educational psychologists such as Benjamin Bloom have shown that people have a specific learning mode. The work of the researchers led by Bloom led to the development of Bloom's Taxonomy which suggests that people have different levels of learning when people are taught new ideas. This work is most often applied to the way in which children are taught in school, and the elementary education worldwide has paid attention to the structure suggested by Bloom where simpler ideas like memorizing the multiplication table is considered to be the first step in learning multiplication before solving complicated mathematical problems that require multiplication. A similar approach can be used to overcome the notion of alienation.

Once an individual is willing to take the steps to overcome the sense of alienation, it is possible to assess one's level of alienation using the AI scale. That information then provides a good picture of the level of alienation from the different components of technology which in turn shows the level of alienation from different kinds of tools. Since the level of alienation is usually not the same across all tools, the user can then decide which particular regimes of alienation require attention and then begin to work on those areas to add to the quality of use of the specific tools. What is critical to overcome the sense of alienation is a desire to do so, and the belief that one can eventually deal with the alien technology.

Notes

1. This quote was extracted from a website called "Automobile History" that provides a folkloric history of the automobile. More information is available at the website by pointing the browser at http://www.motorera.com/history/hist08.htm. The information was extracted from the Internet in 2009.
2. Power steering refers to a system where the steering wheel of a car is connected to the wheels of the car through a hydraulic system that makes it easier to steer the car without the driver having to put in great effort to turn the car, especially when the vehicle is large as in the case of a van.
3. The ideas of alienation are best developed in a series of notes that were never formally published and was called the *Economic and Philosophic Manuscripts of 1844*. The idea of alienation was most carefully developed in these manuscripts and was later included in Marx's best-known work called *Capital*, first published in 1867 and thereafter published in many different languages.
4. The idea of alienation as developed by Freud appears in his best-known work called *Civilization and Its Discontents* that was first published in 1930 in German and thereafter has become a widely published work in many different languages including a version published by Penguin Books.
5. Erich Fromm developed and published his take on alienation in the 1955 book called *The Sane Society* that was published by Henry Holt and Company.
6. The idea of alienation was developed by Durkheim in his book called *Suicide*, published in French in 1897, and available now in many different languages including an English version published in 2007 by Penguin Classics.
7. This quote was extracted from a website called "Rumor Has It" that provides a collection of stories about the way in which people use

different tools. More information is available at the website by pointing the browser at http://www.snopes.com/autos/techno/choke.asp. The information was extracted from the Internet in 2009.

8. Available at http://www.snopes.com/autos/techno/choke.asp. Accessed in 2009.

9. If one were to go by strict scientific evidence of evolution there is actually a clear answer to the chicken and egg question. However, within popular cultural imagination this question acts as a metaphor for conditions where causality is not immediately evident.

10. This statement was obtained from an article written by Geoffrey Thomas in the magazine *Air Transport World*, in March 2005 after the A380 was rolled out in Touluse, France before numerous Chief Executive Officers representing possible customers of the A380 aircraft.

11. This quote was extracted from a website called "PDA Review" that provides reviews of gadgets. This particular review was done by Sam Evans in February 2000. More information is available at the website by pointing the browser at http://www.geek.com/hwswrev/pda/IIIse/palmiiise.htm. The information was extracted from the Internet in 2009.

12. This quote was extracted from a website called "Red Gold: The Epic Story of Blood" that provides information about human blood and the different ways it has been treated. This particular website provided information about the early practices of bloodletting. More information is available at the website by pointing the browser at http://www.pbs.org/wnet/redgold/basics/bloodlettinginstruments.html. The information was extracted from the Internet in 2009.

13. This information was obtained from the article titled "More than just music" that Nicole Garbarni published in *Scientific American*, 291(6): 108–111.

14. This quote was extracted from a website called "Microsoft's Response to the Browser Threat" that provides information about different kinds of vulnerabilities of Web browsers. More information is available at the website by pointing the browser at http://news.findlaw.com/microsoft/5.F.2.a.12.html. The information was extracted from the Internet in 2009.

15. Debbie Farmer does regular commentaries on a variety of topics, and this was obtained from an article titled, "Technology ignorance not so bad", that appeared in *The Campbell Reporter* on August 15, 2001.

16. This quotation was available at a website for the University of California at Berkeley where the Information Services Department offered users advice about the correct way of using e-mail. The material was first

published in March 2004, and was available at http://istpub.berkeley. edu:4201/bcc/Spring2004/updateav.html.

17. This quote was extracted from the website of Fox News Network and referred to an article titled, 'Store Customer Cards a Source for FBI?' written by Kelley Beaucar Vlahos which described the way in which the American Federal Bureau of Investigation planned on using databases to track security threats. More information is available at the website by pointing the browser at http://www.foxnews.com/ story/0,2933,59262,00.html. The information was extracted from the Internet in 2009.

18. This quote was extracted from the website of the Boston Globe newspaper and referred to an article titled, "A wasted opportunity in war on terror," written by Hiawatha Bray which described the way in which different databases can be used for keeping track of people. More information is available at the website by pointing the browser at http://www.boston.com/business/technology/articles/2005/08/15/a_ wasted_opportunity_in_war_on_terror/. The information was extracted from the Internet in 2009.

19. The term microprocessor refers to the main part of any computer and is a tiny device that can process a large amount of data by doing numerous mathematical computations at a very rapid rate.

20. The main passenger cars were the Ambassador that was modeled after a particular Austin design, the Standard Herald designed to be similar to the Triumph, the Fiat made in collaboration with the Italian design, and a few other commercial vehicles.

21. This quote was extracted from the website of the *Pittsburgh Tribune* newspaper and referred to an article titled, "Consumers opt to fix vehicles, not replace them" written by Joe Napsha which described the way in which consumers are opting to repair rather than replace. More information is available at the website by pointing the browser at http://www.pittsburghlive.com/x/pittsburghtrib/business/s_599098. html. The information was extracted from the Internet in 2009.

22. Antonio Gramsci was an Italian intellectual who wrote extensively during his imprisonment in the Fascist prisons during World War II. These were eventually published in 1947 in a book called *The Prison Notebooks*. Much of the ideas of hegemony were developed in this book which is available as a paperback from International Publishers.

23. The idea of the apparatus was suggested in his essay called "Ideology and Ideological State Apparatuses" that was published in English in 1971 in *Lenin and Philosophy and other Essays*, translated by Ben Brewster, and published by London Publishers.

24. This quote was extracted from the website of the *Harvard Business Blog* referred to an article titled, "Why Jargon Feeds on Lazy Minds", which described the way in which specialized language is sometimes used to a point that it makes matter extremely confusing. More information is available at the website by pointing the browser at http://discussionleader.hbsp.com/berkun/2008/08/why-jargon-feeds-on-lazy-minds.html. The information was extracted from the Internet in 2009.

25. The article called "The Next Phage", authored by Elizabeth Svoboda, appeared on March 31, 2009 and describes the way in which phages have become popular in treating some bacterial infections. More information is available by pointing the browser at http://www.popsci.com/scitech/article/2009-03/next-phage?page=6. The information was accessed in 2009.

26. The point was made in an article titled, "Government 'jargon ban' draws mixed response," written and published in March 2009 which described the process used to ensure simplicity of language in government communications. More information is available at the website by pointing the browser at http://www.computerweekly.com/Articles/2009/03/19/235328/government-jargon-ban-draws-mixed-response.htm. The information was extracted from the Internet in 2009.

27. The argument was made in a 2000 article titled, "Co-opting Customer Competence," published in Volume 78 of the journal.

Index

About the Author

Ananda Mitra (Ph.D., University of Illinois at Urbana Champaign, USA) is Chair and Professor in the Department of Communication, Wake Forest University. He received a B.Tech degree from the Indian Institute of Technology at Kharagpur and thereafter an M.A. in communication from Wake Forest University North Carolina, USA.

The primary areas of his teaching and research are: relationships between new media technologies and culture; analysis of media and culture in South Asia; research methodology; critical studies; and recreation and leisure research. He has also served as a consultant to private industries, universities, colleges, and local government agencies across the world. His published works include *Television and Popular Culture in India* (1993), *India through the Western Lens* (1999), *Research Methods in Park, Recreation and Leisure Services* (2000) and the *Digital Life* (2010) series that includes six books on various aspects of the contemporary digital world and numerous scholarly articles in various reputed academic journals.